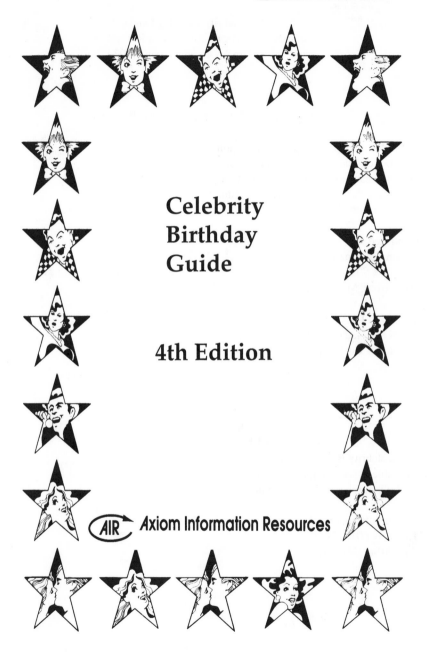

Celebrity
Birthday
Guide

4th Edition

Axiom Information Resources

Celebrity Birthday Guide™
Published by Axiom Information Resources
Ann Arbor, Michigan 48107 USA

Copyright © 1997 Axiom Information Resources

Published by:
Axiom Information Resources
P.O. Box 8015
Ann Arbor, MI 48107

Printed in USA
ISBN #0-943213-25-8
Library of Congress Catalog Card Number 93-77300

SPECIAL SALES
The Celebrity Birthday Guide™ is
available at special quantity discounts
for bulk purchases. For information write:

Axiom Information Resources
P.O. Box 8015-T8
Ann Arbor, MI 48107

January 1

Idi Amin	1/1/25
Dana Andrews	1/1/09
Dennis Archer	1/1/42
Charles Bickford	1/1/1889
Xavier Cugat	1/1/00
E.M. Forster	1/1/1879
Barry Goldwater	1/1/09
Hank Greenberg	1/1/11
Ernest Hollings	1/1/22
J. Edgar Hoover	1/1/1895
Lamarr Hoyt	1/1/55
Carole Landis	1/1/19
Frank Langella	1/1/40
Terry Moore	1/1/32
Don Novello	1/1/43
Paul Revere	1/1/1735
Betsy Ross	1/1/1752
J.D. Salinger	1/1/19
Shelby Steele	1/1/46
Doak Walker	1/1/27

January 2

Isaac Asimov	1/2/20
Jim Bakker	1/2/39
David Cone	1/2/63
William Crowe	1/2/25
Christopher Durang	1/2/49
Cuba Gooding, Jr.	1/2/68
Calvin Hill	1/2/47
Toshiki Kaifu	1/2/31
Julius LaRosa	1/2/30
Edgar Martinez	1/2/63
Roger Miller	1/2/36
Scott Mitchell	1/2/68
Sally Rand	1/2/00
Dan Rostenkowski	1/2/28
Joseph Stalin	1/2/1880
Vera Zorina	1/2/17

January 3

Maxine Andrews	1/3/18
Victor Borge	1/3/09
Dabney Coleman	1/3/32
Marion Davies	1/3/1897
Jim Everett	1/3/63
Millard Fuller	1/3/35
Betty Furness	1/3/16
Mel Gibson	1/3/56
Carla Hills	1/3/34
Bobby Hull	1/3/39
John Paul Jones	1/3/46
David Lloyd	1/3/48
Robert Loggia	1/3/30
Ray Milland	1/3/08
Zasu Pitts	1/3/1898
Victoria Principal	1/3/50
Willie Ribbs	1/3/56
Betty Rollin	1/3/36
Stephen Stills	1/3/45
Hank Stram	1/3/23
John Sturges	1/3/10
J.R.R. Tolkien	1/3/1892
Jesse White	1/3/19
Anna May Wong	1/3/07

January 4

William Bendix	1/4/06
Sorrell Booke	1/4/30
Louis Braille	1/4/1809
Grace Bumbry	1/4/37
Dyan Cannon	1/4/39
George Washington Carver	1/4/1859
Barbara Ann Cochran	1/4/51
Russ Columbo	1/4/08
Matt Frewer	1/4/58
Charlie Hough	1/4/48
Joe Kleine	1/4/62
Cliff Levingston	1/4/61
Patty Loveless	1/4/57
Johnny Lujack	1/4/25
Sir Isaac Newton	1/4/1643
Floyd Patterson	1/4/35
Maureen Reagan	1/4/41
Barbara Rush	1/4/27
Don Shula	1/4/30
Tom Thumb	1/4/1838
Jane Wyman	1/4/14

January 5

Alvin Ailey 1/5/31
Jean-Pierre Aumont 1/5/11
King Juan Carlos 1/5/38
Jeane Dixon 1/5/18
Friedrich Durrenmatt 1/5/21
Robert Duvall 1/5/31
Alex English 1/5/54
Khalil Gibran 1/5/1883
Raisa Gorbachev 1/5/32
Diane Keaton 1/5/46
Chuck Knoll 1/5/32
Ted Lange 1/5/49
Pamela Sue Martin 1/5/54
Walter Mondale 1/5/28
Eugene "Mercury" Morris 1/5/47
Chuck Noll 1/5/31
Charlie Rose 1/5/42
Yves Tanguy 1/5/00
Sam Wyche 1/5/45

January 6

Joey Adams 1/6/11
Capucine 1/6/35
E.L. Doctorow 1/6/31
Bonnie Franklin 1/6/44
Charles Haley 1/6/64
Lou Harris 1/6/21
Lou Holtz 1/6/37
Nancy Lopez 1/6/57
Tom Mix 1/6/1880
Rev. Sun Myung Moon 1/6/20
Carl Sandbury 1/6/1878
Earl Scruggs 1/6/24
John Singleton 1/6/68
Vic Taback 1/6/29
Danny Thomas 1/6/14
Early Wynn 1/6/20
Loretta Young 1/6/13

January 7

Charles Addams 1/7/12
Nicholson Baker 1/7/57
Noah Beery 1/7/1884
William Peter Blatty 1/7/28
Nicolas Cage 1/7/64
Katie Couric 1/7/57
Millard Fillmore 1/7/1800
Vincent Gardenia 1/7/23
Erin Gray 1/7/52
Victor Lasky 1/7/18
Kenny Loggins 1/7/48
Jann Wenner 1/7/47

January 8

Shirley Bassey 1/8/37
David Bowie 1/8/47
Vladimir Feltsman 1/8/52
Jose Ferrer 1/8/12
Little Anthony 1/8/41
Carolina Herrera 1/8/39
Butterfly McQueen 1/8/11
Yvette Mimieux 1/8/41
Charles Osgood 1/8/33
Elvis Presley 1/8/35
Alexandra Ripley 1/8/34
Soupy Sales 1/8/30
Bruce Sutter 1/8/53
Giorgio Tozzi 1/8/23

January 9

Joan Baez 1/9/41
George Balanchine 1/9/04
Vilma Banky 1/9/03
Muggsy Bogues 1/9/65
Simone deBeauvoir 1/9/08
Bob Denver 1/9/35
Crystal Gayle 1/9/51
Earl Graves 1/9/35
Judith Krantz 1/9/28
Franando Lamas 1/9/20
Richard Nixon 1/9/13
Gypsy Rose Lee 1/9/14
Bart Starr 1/9/34
Lee Van Cleef 1/9/25
Susannah York 1/9/42

January 10

Noah Beery, Jr	1/10/16
Pat Benatar	1/10/52
Ray Bolger	1/10/04
Donald Brooks	1/10/28
Francis X. Bushman	1/10/1883
Jim Croce	1/10/43
Meyer Davis	1/10/1893
George Forman	1/10/49
Paul Henreid	1/10/08
Gisele Mackenzie	1/10/27
Willie McCovey	1/10/38
Sherrill Milnes	1/10/35
Sal Mineo	1/10/39
Johnny Ray	1/10/27
Glen Robinson	1/10/73
Rod Stewart	1/10/45

January 11

Mary J. Blige	1/11/71
Monte Blue	1/11/1890
Clarence Clemons	1/11/42
Ben Crenshaw	1/11/52
Darryl Dawkins	1/11/57
Cris Ford	1/11/49
Alexander Hamilton	1/11/1757
Naomi Judd	1/11/46
Eva La Gallienne	1/11/1899
Rod Taylor	1/11/30
Grant Tinker	1/11/26
David Wolper	1/11/28

January 12

Kirstie Alley	1/12/55
Anthony Andrews	1/12/48
P.W. Botha	1/12/16
Joe Frazier	1/12/44
John Hancock	1/12/1736
Patsy Kelly	1/12/10
Kreskin	1/12/35
Rush Limbaugh	1/12/51
Jack London	1/12/1876
Ray Price	1/12/26
Luise Rainer	1/12/12
Tex Ritter	1/12/07
Howard Stern	1/12/54
Ricky Van Shelton	1/12/52
Vendela	1/12/67
Dominque Wilkins	1/12/60
Henry Youngman	1/12/06

January 13

Horatio Alger	1/13/1832
Sandra Church	1/13/43
Alfred Fuller	1/13/1885
Julia Louis-Dreyfus	1/13/61
Jay McInerney	1/13/55
Penelope Ann Miller	1/13/64
Gary Moore	1/13/15
Charles Nelson Reilly	1/13/31
Robert Stack	1/13/19
Frances Sternhagen	1/13/30
Potter Stewart	1/13/15
Brandon Tartikoff	1/13/49
Sophie Tucker	1/13/1884
Gwen Verdon	1/13/25

January 14

Benedict Arnold	1/14/1741
Jason Bateman	1/14/69
Cecil Beaton	1/14/04
Julian Bond	1/14/40
Bebe Daniels	1/14/01
Faye Dunaway	1/14/41
Marjoe Gortner	1/14/44
Morihiro Hosokawa	1/14/38
L.L. Cool J.	1/14/68
Lawrence Kasdan	1/14/49
John Dos Passos	1/14/1896
Hal Roach	1/14/1892
Andy Rooney	1/14/19
Albert Schweitzer	1/14/1875
Steven Soderbergh	1/14/63
Nina Totenberg	1/14/44
Thomas Tryson	1/14/26
Carl Weathers	1/14/47

January 15

Martin Agronsky 1/15/15
Lloyd Bridges 1/15/13
Charo 1/15/51
Delion DeShields 1/15/69
Kenny Easley 1/15/59
Stuart Eizenstat 1/15/43
Ernest Gaines 1/15/33
Ace Goodman 1/15/1899
Martin Luther King, Jr 1/15/29
Moliere 1/15/1622
Margaret O'Brien 1/15/37
Cardinal John O'Connor 1/15/20
Mary Pierce 1/15/75
Maria Schell 1/15/26
Edwin Sherin 1/15/30
Edward Teller 1/15/08
Lee Teng-hui 1/15/23

January 16

Debbie Allen 1/16/50
John H. Carpenter 1/16/48
Dizzy Dean 1/16/11
A.J. Foyt 1/16/35
Marilyn Horne 1/16/34
Alexander Knox 1/16/07
Ethel Merman 1/16/09
Ronnie Milsap 1/16/44
Kate Moss 1/16/74
Sade 1/16/60
Francesco Scavullo 1/16/29
Stirling Silliphant 1/16/18
Michael Wilding, Jr 1/16/33

January 17

Muhammad Ali 1/17/42
Al Capone 1/17/1899
Jim Carrey 1/17/62
David Caruso 1/17/56
Chili Davis 1/17/60
Steve Earle 1/17/55
Buzz Feitshans 1/17/37
Benjamin Franklin 1/17/1706
James Earl Jones 1/17/31

Andy Kaufman 1/17/49
Jerome Kern 1/17/1885
Shari Lewis 1/17/34
Billy R. Moses 1/17/59
Sheree North 1/17/33
Maury Povich 1/17/39
Vidal Sasson 1/17/28
Mack Sennett 1/17/1884
Moira Shearer 1/17/26
Mick Taylor 1/17/48
Paul Young 1/17/56
Betty White 1/17/17
Douglas Wilder 1/17/31
Don Zimmer 1/17/31

January 18

John Boorman 1/18/33
Jacob Bronowski 1/18/08
Kevin Costner 1/18/55
Curt Flood 1/18/38
Bobby Goldsboro 1/18/41
Cary Grant 1/18/04
Oliver Hardy 1/18/1892
Danny Kaye 1/18/13
Mark Messier 1/18/61
Peter Mark Roger 1/18/1779
David Ruffin 1/18/41
Daniel Webster 1/18/1782

January 19

O.J. Anderson 1/19/57
Desi Arnaz, Jr. 1/19/53
Michael Crawford 1/19/42
Stefan Edberg 1/19/66
Shelley Fabares 1/19/44
Tippi Hedren 1/19/35
Oveta Culp Hobby 1/19/05
John H. Johnson 1/19/18
Janis Joplin 1/19/43
Robert E. Lee 1/19/1807
Richard Lester 1/19/32
Robert MacNeil 1/19/31
Guy Madison 1/19/22
Robert Palmer 1/19/49

Dolly Parton 1/19/46
Edgar Allen Poe 1/19/1809
John Raitt 1/19/17
Dan Reeves 1/19/44
Junior Seau 1/19/69
Jean Stapleton 1/19/23
Fritz Weaver 1/19/26

January 20
Jay Adamson 1/20/00
Edwin "Buzz" Aldrin 1/20/30
Leon Ames 1/20/03
George Burns 1/20/1896
Federico Fellini 1/20/20
Ozzie Guillen 1/20/64
Ron Harper 1/20/64
DeForest Kelley 1/20/20
Lorenzo Lamas 1/20/58
Ely Landau 1/20/20
Leadbelly 1/20/1888
David Lynch 1/20/46
Patricia Neal 1/20/26
Aristotle Onassis 1/20/06
Dorothy Provine 1/20/37
Paul Stanley 1/20/52
Slim Whitman 1/20/24

January 21
Akeem Abdul Olajuwon 1/21/64
Robby Benson 1/21/57
John Moses Browning 1/21/1854
Geena Davis 1/21/57
Mac Davis 1/21/42
Christian Dior 1/21/05
Placido Domingo 1/21/41
Richie Havens 1/21/41
Benny Hill 1/21/25
Wolfman Jack 1/21/38
Stonewall Jackson 1/21/1824
J. Carrol Naish 1/21/00
Jack Nicklaus 1/21/40
Johnny Oates 1/21/46
Telly Savalas 1/21/24
Detlet Schrempf 1/21/63

Paul Scofield 1/21/22

January 22
Ross Barnett 1/22/1898
Birch Bayh 1/22/28
Bill Bixby 1/22/34
Linda Blair 1/22/59
Mike Bossy 1/22/57
Benjamin Chavis 1/22/48
Sam Cooke 1/22/31
Quintin Dailey 1/22/61
Teddy Gentry 1/22/52
D.W. Griffith 1/22/1875
Lester Hayes 1/22/55
John Hurt 1/22/40
Piper Laurie 1/22/32
Steve Perry 1/22/49
George Seifert 1/22/40
Ann Sothern 1/22/09
August Strindberg 1/22/1849
U Thant 1/22/09
Conrad Veidt 1/22/1893
Joseph Wambaugh 1/22/37
William Warfield 1/22/20

January 23
Richard Dean Anderson 1/23/50
Prinesss Caroline 1/23/57
Dan Duryea 1/23/07
Sergei Eisenstein 1/23/1898
Gil Gerard 1/23/43
Rutger Hauer 1/23/44
Ernie Kovaks 1/23/19
Edouard Manet 1/23/1832
Jeanne Moreau 1/23/28
Franklin Pangborn 1/23/1893
Chita Rivera 1/23/33
Randolph Scott 1/23/1898
Bob Steele 1/23/1893
Sharon Tate 1/23/43

January 24
Tatyana M. Ali 1/24/79
Roger Baldwin 1/24/1884

Bobby Beathard 1/24/37
John Belush 1/24/49
Ernest Borgnine 1/24/17
Jack Brickhouse 1/24/16
Jerry Burns 1/24/27
Neil Diamond 1/24/41
Mark Eaton 1/24/57
Leonard Goldberg 1/24/34
Mark Goodson 1/24/15
Nastassia Kinski 1/24/60
Julian Krainin 1/24/41
Bernard Kroger 1/24/1860
Desmond Morris 1/24/28
Michael Ontkean 1/24/50
Mary Lou Retton 1/24/68
Oral Roberts 1/24/18
Yakov Smirnoff 1/24/51
Maria Tallchief 1/24/25
Edith Wharton 1/24/1862
Estelle Winwood 1/24/1883

January 25

Elizabeth Allen 1/25/34
Corazon Aquino 1/25/33
Mildred Dunnock 1/25/06
Mark Duper 1/25/59
Hal Gurnee 1/25/35
Ernie Harwell 1/25/18
Dean Jones 1/25/36
Larry Kramer 1/25/35
Somerset Maugham 1/25/1874
Chris Mills 1/25/70
Gloria Naylor 1/25/50
Edwin Newman 1/25/19
Greg Palmer 1/25/27
Eduard Shevardnadze 1/25/28
Leigh Taylor-Young 1/25/44

January 26

Anita Baker 1/26/58
Angela Davis 1/26/44
Ellen DeGeneres 1/26/58
Jules Feiffer 1/26/29
Scott Glenn 1/26/42

Wayne Gretzky 1/26/61
Anne Jeffreys 1/26/23
Eartha Kitt 1/26/28
Joan Leslie 1/26/25
Douglas MacArthur 1/26/1880
Paul Newman 1/26/25
Gene Siskel 1/26/46
Bob Uecker 1/26/35
Roger Vadim 1/26/28
Eddie Van Halen 1/26/57
Jimmy Van Heusen 1/26/13

January 27

Bobby "Blue" Bland 1/27/30
Lewis Carroll 1/27/1832
Cris Collinsworth 1/27/59
Troy Donahue 1/27/37
Bridget Fonda 1/27/64
Samuel Gompers 1/27/18
Brian Gottfried 1/27/52
William Randolph Hearst, Jr. ... 1/27/08
Skitch Henderson 1/27/18
Tracy Lawrence 1/27/68
Wolfgang Amadeus Mozart 1/27/1756
Donna Reed 1/27/21
Mordecai Richler 1/27/31
Hyman Rickover 1/27/00
Mimi Rogers 1/27/56
Anne Rudin 1/27/24
Ingrid Thulin 1/27/29

January 28

Alan Alda 1/28/36
Mikhail Baryshnikov 1/28/48
Barbi Benton 1/28/50
Susan Howard 1/28/43
Martha Keller 1/28/44
Claes Oldenburg 1/28/29
Jackson Pollock 1/28/12
Nicholas Price 1/28/57
Arthur Rubinstein 1/28/1887
Susan Sontag 1/28/33
Bill White 1/28/34
Elijah Wood 1/28/81

January 29

"Paddy" Chayefsky 1/29/23
Ann Compton 1/29/47
Phil Everly 1/29/39
W.C. Fields 1/29/1880
John Forsythe 1/29/18
Sara Gilbert 1/29/75
Germaine Greer 1/29/39
Ann Jillian 1/29/51
Stacey King 1/29/67
Claudine Longet 1/29/42
Greg Louganis 1/29/60
Victor Mature 1/29/16
Andre Reed 1/29/64
Katharine Ross 1/29/43
Tom Selleck 1/29/45
Oprah Winfrey 1/29/54

January 30

Marty Balin 1/30/42
Richard Cheney 1/30/41
Phil Collins 1/30/51
Tammy Grimes 1/30/36
Gene Hackman 1/30/31
John Ireland 1/30/15
Sharon Pratt Kelly 1/30/44
Dorothy Malone 1/30/25
Delbert Mann 1/30/20
Hugh Marlowe 1/30/14
Dick Martin 1/30/32
Harold Prince 1/30/28
Vanessa Redgrave 1/30/37
Franklin Roosevelt 1/30/1882
Louis Rukeyser 1/30/33
Boris Spassky 1/30/37
Payne Stewart 1/30/57
Curtis Strange 1/30/55
Mychal Thompson 1/30/55

January 31

Tallulah Bankhead 1/31/03
Ernie Banks 1/31/31
Eddie Cantor 1/31/1892

Carol Channing 1/31/23
Joanne Dru 1/31/23
James Franciscus 1/31/34
Richard Gephart 1/31/41
Philip Glass 1/31/37
Zane Grey 1/31/1875
Benjamin Hooks 1/31/25
Mario Lanza 1/31/21
Norman Mailer 1/31/23
Lynn Neary 1/31/50
John O'Hara 1/31/05
Suzanne Pleshette 1/31/37
Jackie Robinson 1/31/19
Nolan Ryan 1/31/47
Jean Simmons 1/31/29
Alfred Taubman 1/31/25
Jersey Joe Walcott 1/31/14
Jessica Walter 1/31/44
James Watts 1/31/38

February 1

Don Everly 2/1/37
John Ford 2/1/1895
Clark Gable 2/1/01
Sherman Hemsley 2/1/38
Hildegrade 2/1/06
Langston Hughes 2/1/02
Rick James 2/1/48
Terry Jones 2/1/42
Matt Lattanzi 2/1/59
Garrett Morris 2/1/37
S.J. Perelman 2/1/04
Lisa Marie Presley 2/1/68
Bob Shane 2/1/34
Paula Shore 2/1/70
Anastaslo Somoza 2/1/1896
Princess Stephanie 2/1/65
Renata Tebaldi 2/1/22
Jim Thorpe (Golfer) 2/1/49
Stuart Whitman 2/1/26
Boris Yeltsin 2/1/31

February 2

Christie Brinkley 2/2/53

James Dickey 2/2/23
Barry Diller 2/2/42
Vlade Divac 2/2/68
Abba Eban 2/2/15
Sean Elliott 2/2/68
Simon Estes 2/2/38
Farrah Fawcett 2/2/47
Stan Getz 2/2/27
Gale Gordon 2/2/06
L.C. Greenwood 2/2/49
George Halas 2/2/1895
Jascha Heifetz 2/2/01
Bo Hopkins 2/2/42
James Joyce 2/2/1882
Burton Lane 2/2/12
Robert Mandan 2/2/32
Dexter Manley 2/2/59
Graham Nash 2/2/42
Gustavus Ramsay 2/2/37
Ayn Rand 2/2/05
S.Z. Sakall 2/2/1884
Stefan Schnabel 2/2/12
Liz Smith 2/2/23
Tom Smothers 2/2/37
Elaine Stritch 2/2/28
Danny White 2/2/52

February 3

Paul Auster 2/3/47
Shelly Berman 2/3/26
Joey Bishop 2/3/18
Victor Buono 2/3/38
Blythe Danner 2/3/43
Morgan Fairchild 2/3/50
Bob Griese 2/3/45
Kathleen Kinmont 2/3/67
Fred Lynn 2/3/52
James Michener 2/3/07
Norman Rockwell 2/3/1894
Fran Tarkenton 2/3/40

February 4

Conrad Bain 2/4/23
Clint Black 2/4/62

David Brenner 2/4/45
Bobby Brown 2/4/69
Alice Cooper 2/4/48
Lisa Eichhorn 2/4/52
Betty Friedan 2/4/21
Erich Leinsdorf 2/4/12
Charles Lindbergh 2/4/02
Ida Lupino 2/4/18
Rosa Parks 2/4/13
Dan Quayle 2/4/47
Lawrence Taylor 2/4/59

February 5

Hank Aaron 2/5/34
Roberto Alomar 2/5/68
William Burrows 2/5/14
Red Button 2/5/19
Stephen Cannell 2/5/41
John Carradine 2/5/06
Stuart Damon 2/5/37
Val Dufour 2/5/27
Andrew Greeley 2/5/28
Christopher Guest 2/5/48
Barbara Hershey 2/5/48
Tim Holt 2/5/18
Jennifer Jason Leigh 2/5/62
Charlotte Rampling 2/5/46
Roger Staubach 2/5/42
Adlai Stevenson, Jr. 2/5/00
Arthur Ochs Sulzberger 2/5/26
Darrell Waltrip 2/5/47

February 6

Tom Brokaw 2/6/40
Natalie Cole 2/6/49
Larry "Buster" Crabbe 2/6/08
Fabian 2/6/43
Mike Farrell 2/6/39
Zsa Zsa Gabor 2/6/19
Gayle Hunnicutt 2/6/43
Patrick MacNee 2/6/22
Louis Nizer 2/6/02
Ramon Novarro 2/6/1899
Gigi Perreau 2/6/41

Ronald Reagan 2/6/11
Axl Rose 2/6/62
Babe Ruth 2/6/1895
Rip Torn 2/6/31
Robert Townsend 2/6/57
Francois Truffaut 2/6/32
Mamie Van Doren 2/6/33

February 7

Leon Bibb 2/7/22
Eubie Blakes 2/7/1883
Eddie Bracken 2/7/20
Keefe Brasselle 2/7/23
Garth Brooks 2/7/62
John Deere 2/7/1804
Charles Dickens 2/7/1812
Frederick Douglass 2/7/1817
Juliette Greco 2/7/27
Burt Hooton 2/7/50
Juwan Howard 2/7/73
Sinclair Lewis 2/7/1885
Josef Mengele 2/7/11
Dan Quisenberry 2/7/54
Chris Rock 2/7/66
James Spader 2/7/60
Gay Talese 2/7/32

February 8

Brooke Adams 2/8/49
Gary Coleman 2/8/68
James Dean 2/8/31
Dame Edith Evans 2/8/1888
John Grisham 2/8/55
Robert Klein 2/8/42
Ted Koppel 2/8/40
Jack Lemmon 2/8/25
Adolphe Menjou 2/8/1890
Alonzo Mourning 2/8/70
Nick Nolte 2/8/42
William Tecumseh Sherman .. 2/8/1820
Lana Turner 2/8/20
Jules Verne 2/8/1828
King Vidor 2/8/1894
John Williams 2/8/32

February 9

Sy Barry 2/9/44
Brendan Behan 2/9/23
Ronald Coleman 2/9/1891
Brian Donlevy 2/9/1899
Mia Farrow 2/9/45
Kathryn Grayson 2/9/23
Carole King 2/9/41
John Kruk 2/9/61
Judith Light 2/9/50
Carmen Miranda 2/9/09
Roger Mudd 2/9/28
Joe Pesci 2/9/43
Dean Rusk 2/9/09
Travis Tritt 2/9/64
Ernest Tubb 2/9/14
Bill Veeck 2/9/14
Alice Walker 2/9/44
Albert Wasserman 2/9/21
Peggy Wood 2/9/1892

February 10

Larry Adler 2/10/14
Stella Adler 2/10/02
Judith Anderson 2/10/1898
Bertolt Brecht 2/10/1898
Lon Chaney, Jr. 2/10/05
Donovan 2/10/46
Jimmy Durante 2/10/1893
Len Dykstra 2/10/63
John Farrow 2/10/06
Roberta Flack 2/10/40
Dennis Gentry 2/10/59
Alan Hale 2/10/1892
Greg Norman 2/10/55
Leontyne Price 2/10/27
Mark Spitz 2/10/50
George Stephanopolos 2/10/61
Bill Tilden 2/10/1893
Robert Wagner 2/10/30

February 11

Max Baer 2/11/09
Lloyd Bentsen 2/11/21

Paul Bocuse 2/11/26
Thomas Edison 2/11/1847
Eva Gabor. 2/11/25
Tina Louise 2/11/37
Joseph Mankiewicz 2/11/09
Virgina Masters 2/11/25
Sergio Mendes 2/11/41
Leslie Nielsen 2/11/26
Boris Pasternak 2/11/1890
Burt Reynolds 2/11/36
Sidney Sheldon 2/11/17
Kim Stanley 2/11/25
Jane Yolen 2/11/39

February 12

Maud Adams 2/12/45
Susan Anton 2/12/50
Joe Don Baker 2/12/36
Ted Benecke 2/12/14
Judy Blume 2/12/38
Gen. Omar Bradley 2/12/1893
Charles Darwin 2/12/1809
Dom Dimaggio 2/12/17
Joe Garagiola 2/12/26
Lorne Greene 2/12/15
Arsenio Hall 2/12/56
Joanna Kerns 2/12/53
Abraham Lincoln 2/12/1809
Richard Lutz 2/12/32
Ted Mack 2/12/04
Larry Nance 2/12/59
Chynna Phillips 2/12/68
Eddie Robinson 2/12/19
Bill Russell 2/12/34
Johnny Rutherford 2/12/38
Paul Shenar 2/12/36
Arlen Specter 2/12/30
Forrest Tucker 2/12/19
Franco Zeffirelli 2/12/23

February 13

Stockard Channing 2/13/44
Eileen Farrell 2/13/20
"Tennessee" Ernie Ford 2/13/19

Peter Gabriel 2/13/50
Carol Lynley 2/13/43
David Naughton 2/13/51
Kim Novak 2/13/33
Oliver Reed 2/13/38
George Segal 2/13/34
Bo Svenson 2/13/41
Peter Tork 2/13/44
Grant Wood 2/13/1892
Gen. Chuck Yeager 2/13/23

February 14

Mel Allen 2/14/13
Jack Benny 2/14/1894
Carl Bernstein 2/14/44
Drew Bledsoe 2/14/72
Joan Carew Crosby 2/14/34
Hugh Downs 2/14/21
Stu Erwin 2/14/02
Peter Gimbel 2/14/28
Florence Henderson 2/14/34
Frank Harris 2/14/1856
Woody Hayes 2/14/13
Gregory Hines 2/14/46
Jimmy Hoffa 2/14/13
Jim Kelly 2/14/60
Vic Morrow 2/14/32
Alan Parker 2/14/44
Andrew Prine 2/14/36
Thelma Ritter 2/14/05
Teller 2/14/48
Paul Tsongas 2/14/41
Ken Wahl 2/14/60

February 15

(Adolfo) F. Sardina 2/15/33
John Anderson 2/15/22
Susan B. Anthony 2/15/1820
Harold Arlen 2/15/05
John Barrymore 2/15/1882
Marisa Berenson 2/15/48
Clair Bloom 2/15/31
Yelena Bonner 2/15/23
Susan Brownmiller 2/15/35

Anthony Burgess 2/15/17
Ron Cey 2/15/48
Roger B. Chaffee 2/15/35
Tim Cheveldae 2/15/68
Galileo 2/15/1564
Matt Groening 2/15/54
Brian Holland 2/15/41
Jaromir Jagr 2/15/72
Harvey Korman 2/15/27
Melisse Manchester 2/15/51
Kevin McCarthy 2/15/14
Cesar Romero 2/15/07
James Schlesinger 2/15/29
Jane Seymour 2/15/51
Gale Sondergaard 2/15/1899
Art Spiegelman 2/15/48
Charles Lewis Tiffany 2/15/1812

February 16
Patti Andrews 2/16/20
Brian Bedford 2/16/35
Edgar Bergen 2/16/03
Jerome Bettis 2/16/72
Sonny Bono 2/16/40
LeVar Burton 2/16/57
Tracy Carter 2/16/40
Katherine Cornell 2/16/1898
James Ingram 2/16/56
William Katt 2/16/51
John McEnroe 2/16/59
Chester Morris 2/16/01
Mark Price 2/16/64
John Schlesinger 2/16/26
Andy Taylor 2/16/61
Vera-Ellen 2/16/26
Jimmy Walker 2/16/14

February 17
Marian Anderson 2/17/02
Red Barber 2/17/08
Alan Bates 2/17/34
Mary Frances Berry 2/17/38
Jim Brown 2/17/36
Buster Crabbe 2/17/06

Roger Craig (Mgr.) 2/17/30
Wayne Fontes 2/17/39
Dennis Green 2/17/49
Hal Holbrook 2/17/25
H.L. Hunt 2/17/1889
Tom Jones 2/17/28
Michael Jordan 2/17/63
Arthur Kennedy 2/17/14
Mary Ann Mobley 2/17/39
Wayne Morris 2/17/14
Huey P. Newton 2/17/42
Lou Diamond Phillips 2/17/62
Ruth Rendell 2/17/30
Buddy Ryan 2/17/34
Margaret Truman 2/17/24
Montgomery Ward 2/17/1843

February 18
Sholem Aleichem 2/18/1859
Jean Auel 2/18/36
Helen Gurley Brown 2/18/22
Dane Clark 2/18/13
Bill Cullen 2/18/20
Sinead Cusack 2/18/48
Len Deighton 2/18/29
Billy DeWolfe 2/18/07
Matt Dillon 2/18/64
Milos Forman 2/18/32
Johnny Hart 2/18/31
George Kennedy 2/18/25
Toni Morrison 2/18/31
Manny Mota 2/18/38
Michael Nader 2/18/45
Yoko Ono 2/18/33
Jack Palance 2/18/20
Molly Ringwald 2/18/68
Andres Segovia 2/18/1894
Cybill Shepherd 2/18/50
Georges Simenon 2/18/03
John Travolta 2/18/54
John Warner 2/18/27
Vanna White 2/18/57
Wendell Willkie 2/18/1892
Gahan Wilson 2/18/30

13

February 19

Prince Andrew	2/19/60
Eddie Arcaro	2/19/16
Justine Bateman	2/19/66
Louis Calhern	2/19/1895
John Frankenheim	2/19/30
Cedric Hardwicke	2/19/1893
Stan Kenton	2/19/12
Hana Mandlikova	2/19/62
Lee Marvin	2/19/24
Carson McCullers	2/19/17
Merle Oberon	2/19/11
Smokey Robinson	2/19/40
Dave Stewart	2/19/57
Amy Tan	2/19/52

February 20

Ansel Adams	2/20/02
Edward Albert	2/20/51
Robert B. Altman	2/20/25
Charles Barkley	2/20/63
Amanda Blake	2/20/31
Cindy Crawford	2/20/66
Hugh Culverhouse	2/20/19
Anthony Davis	2/20/51
Sandy Duncan	2/20/46
Christoph Eschenbach	2/20/40
Phil Esposito	2/20/42
J. Geils	2/20/46
Patty Hearst	2/20/54
Mike Leigh	2/20/43
Jennifer O'Neil	2/20/49
Sidney Poitier	2/20/27
Buffy Sainte-Marie	2/20/41
Peter Strauss	2/20/47
Ivana Trump	2/20/49
Bobby Unser	2/20/34
Gloria Vanderbilt	2/20/24
Nancy Wilson	2/20/37

February 21

Christopher Atkins	2/21/61
W.H. Auden	2/21/07
Richard Beymer	2/21/39
Erma Bombeck	2/21/27
Mary-Chapin Carpenter	2/21/58
Jack Coleman	2/21/58
Tricia Nixon-Cox	2/21/46
Tyne Daly	2/21/44
Hubert DeGivenchy	2/21/27
Jill Eikenberry	2/21/47
David Geffen	2/21/43
Barbara Jordan	2/21/36
John Lewis	2/21/40
Gary Lockwood	2/21/37
Rue McClanahan	2/21/34
Guy Mitchell	2/21/27
Robert Mugabe	2/21/24
Anais Nin	2/21/03
Sam Peckinpah	2/21/25
Ann Sheridan	2/21/15
Nina Simone	2/21/33
Olympia J. Snowe	2/21/47

February 22

Amy Alcott	2/22/56
George "Sparky" Anderson	2/22/34
Drew Barrymore	2/22/75
Luis Bunuel	2/22/00
Michael Chang	2/22/72
Frederic Chopin	2/22/1810
Jonathan Demme	2/22/44
Julius Erving	2/22/50
Charles Finley	2/22/18
Edward Gorey	2/22/25
Bunker Hunt	2/22/26
Edward Kennedy	2/22/32
Niki Lauda	2/22/49
Sybil Leek	2/22/17
Sheldon Leonard	2/22/07
Kyle MacLachlan	2/22/59
Edna St. Vincent Millay	2/22/1892
Sir John Mills	2/22/08
Marni Nixon	2/22/30
Sean O'Faolain	2/22/00
George Washington	2/22/1732
Bud Yorkin	2/22/26

Robert Young 2/22/07

February 23
Bobby Bonilla 2/23/63
Silvia Chase......................... 2/23/38
Hal Cooper.......................... 2/23/23
W.E.B. DuBois 2/23/1868
Victor Fleming 2/23/1883
Peter Fonda 2/23/39
Jon Hall.............................. 2/23/13
George Fredrick Handel 2/23/1685
Ed "Too Tall" Jones 2/23/51
Howard Jones 2/23/55
Tom Osborne 2/23/37
William Shirer 2/23/04
Louis Stokes......................... 2/23/25
Helen Sukova 2/23/65
Norman Taurog 2/23/1899
Johnny Winter 2/23/44

February 24
Ted Arison 2/24/24
Barry Bostwick 2/24/45
James Farentino.................... 2/24/38
Mike Fratello........................ 2/24/47
Rupert Holmes 2/24/47
Winslow Homer................... 2/24/1836
Michel Legrand 2/24/32
Joseph Lieberman 2/24/42
Majorie Main 2/24/1890
Eddie Murray 2/24/56
David Newman...................... 2/24/32
Edward James Olmos.............. 2/24/47
Jay Sandrich 2/24/32
Zachary Scott........................ 2/24/14
Renata Scotto 2/24/34
Richard Shull 2/24/29
Abe Vigoda 2/24/21
Heather Whitestone................ 2/24/73
Paula Zahn........................... 2/24/56

February 25
Sean Astin 2/25/71
Diane Baker 2/25/38

Enrico Caruso 2/25/1873
Tom Courtenay 2/25/37
Adelle Davis 2/25/04
Larry Gelbart 2/25/25
George Harrison 2/25/43
Victor Hugo 2/25/1802
Lisa Kirk 2/25/25
"Zeppo" Marx 2/25/01
Tommy Newsom 2/25/29
David Puttnam 2/25/41
Kurt Rambis......................... 2/25/58
Sally Jessy Raphael 2/25/43
Auguste Renoir 2/25/1841
Bobby Riggs 2/25/18
Bob Schieffer........................ 2/25/34
Richard Stern 2/25/28
Faron Young 2/25/34

February 26
Mason Adams 2/26/19
Robert Alda.......................... 2/26/14
Michael Bolton 2/26/53
Godfrey Cambridge................. 2/26/33
Johnny Cash.......................... 2/26/32
"Buffalo Bill" Cody 2/26/1846
Fats Domino 2/26/28
Marshall Faulk 2/26/73
William Frawley.................... 2/26/1893
Jackie Gleason 2/26/16
Whitey Herzog 2/26/31
Betty Hutton 2/26/21
Brian Jones 2/26/43
Margaret Leighton 2/26/22
Priscilla Lopez 2/26/48
Fard Muhammad 2/26/1877
Robert Novak 2/26/31
Tony Randall 2/26/24

February 27
Barbara Badcock 2/27/37
Joan Bennett......................... 2/27/10
Raymond Berry 2/27/33
Greg Caderet 2/27/62
Chelsea Clinton 2/27/80

John Connally 2/27/17
William Demarest 2/27/1892
James T. Farrell 2/27/04
Mary Frann 2/27/43
Mirella Freni 2/27/35
Howard Hesseman 2/27/40
Janet MacLachian 2/27/46
Ralph Nader 2/27/34
David Sarnoff 2/27/1891
John Steinbeck 2/27/02
Elizabeth Taylor 2/27/32
Franchot Tone.......................... 2/27/05
Joanne Woodward 2/27/30
James Worthy 2/27/61

February 28

Svetlana Alliuyeva 2/28/26
Mario Andretti 2/28/40
Stephanie Beacham 2/28/47
Milton Caniff 2/28/07
Adrian Dantley 2/28/56
Charles Durning....................... 2/28/23
John Fahey 2/28/39
Hayden Fry 2/28/29
Gavin MacLeod 2/28/30
Vincente Minnelli..................... 2/28/13
Zero Mostel 2/28/15
Vaslav Nijinsky 2/28/1890
Linus Pauling 2/28/01
Bernardetts Peters 2/28/48
Molly Picon 2/28/1898
Bugsy Siegel.............................. 2/28/06
Bubba Smith 2/28/45
Dean Smith 2/28/31
Tommy Tune 2/28/39
John Turturro 2/28/57

February 29

Betty Ackerman 2/29/28
Joss Akland 2/29/28
Jimmy Dorsey........................... 2/29/04
Dennis Farina 2/29/44
Arthur Franz............................. 2/29/20
Phyllis Frelich 2/29/44

Jack Lousma 2/29/30
Michele Morgan 2/29/20
Jean Negulesco 2/29/00
Alex Rocco 2/29/36
Al Rosen 2/29/24
Gioacchino Rossini 2/29/1792
Willi Smith 2/29/48
William Wellman 2/29/1896

March 1

Lionel Atwill........................... 3/1/1885
Catherine Bach 3/1/54
Harry Belafonte 3/1/27
Dirk Benedict............................. 3/1/44
Harry Caray 3/1/19
Robert Clary 3/1/26
Robert Conrad 3/1/35
Terence Cardinal Cooke 3/1/21
Roger Daltrey 3/1/44
Timothy Daly 3/1/56
Joan Hackett 3/1/42
Ron Howard 3/1/54
Nik Kershaw 3/1/58
Glenn Miller............................... 3/1/04
David Niven 3/1/10
Yitzhak Rabin 3/1/22
Judith Rossner 3/1/35
Pete Rozell................................. 3/1/26
Raymond Saint Jacques............. 3/1/30
Dinah Shore 3/1/21
Donald Slayton........................... 3/1/24
Alan Thicke................................. 3/1/48
Chris Webber.............................. 3/1/73

March 2

Desi Arnaz 3/2/17
Jon Bon Jovi 3/2/61
Gate Brown 3/2/39
Karen Carpenter........................ 3/2/50
Denny Crum 3/2/37
John Cullum 3/2/30
Mikhail Gorbachev 3/2/31

Sam Houston 3/2/1793
John Irvin 3/2/42
Jennifer Jones 3/2/19
Laraine Newman 3/2/52
Jay Osmond 3/2/55
Lou Reed 3/2/44
Dr. Seuss 3/2/04
Gene Stallings 3/2/35
Peter Straub 3/2/43
Al Waxman 3/2/35
Kurt Weill................................... 3/2/00
Tom Wolfe 3/2/31
Ian Woosnam.............................. 3/2/58

March 3
Adrian... 3/3/03
Diana Barrymore........................ 3/3/21
Bobby Driscoll 3/3/36
Perry Ellis.................................. 3/3/40
David Faustin 3/3/74
Alexander Graham Bell 3/3/1847
Jean Harlow 3/3/11
Jackie Joyner-Kersee................... 3/3/62
Ring Lardner 3/3/1885
Ed Marinaro............................... 3/3/50
Rick Mirer 3/3/70
Lee Radziwell 3/3/33
Miranda Richardson................... 3/3/58
Matthew Ridgway 3/3/1895
Gia Scala 3/3/34
Tone-Loc..................................... 3/3/66
Herschell Walker 3/3/62

March 4
Chastity Bono 3/4/69
John Garfield 3/4/13
Charles Goren............................. 3/4/01
Kevin Johnson 3/4/66
Patsy Kensit 3/4/68
Kay Lenz 3/4/53
Kevin Loughery 3/4/40
Miriam Makeba.......................... 3/4/32
Ray "Boom Boom" Mancini 3/4/61
Barbara McNair.......................... 3/4/37

Catherine O'Hara 3/4/54
Paula Prentiss 3/4/39
Knute Rockne 3/4/1888
Chris Squire 3/4/48
Bobby Womack 3/4/44

March 5
Rocky Bleier................................ 3/5/46
Jack Cassidy................................ 3/5/27
Virginia Field Christine 3/5/20
Samantha Eggar 3/5/40
Eugene Fodor 3/5/50
Andy Gibb 3/5/58
Rex Harrison............................... 3/5/08
Michael Irving 3/5/66
Lorin Maazel.............................. 3/5/30
Michelangelo 3/5/1475
James Nobel................................ 3/5/22
Pier Paolo Pasolini 3/5/22
Scott Skiles 3/5/64
Dean Stockwell........................... 3/5/36
Niki Taylor................................. 3/5/75
Laurence Tisch 3/5/23
Marsha Warfield 3/5/54
Michael Warren.......................... 3/5/46
Fred Williamson......................... 3/5/38

March 6
Tom Arnold 3/6/59
Marion Barry 3/6/36
Sarah Caldwell 3/6/24
L. Gordon Cooper 3/6/27
Lou Costello................................ 3/6/08
Will Eisner.................................. 3/6/17
Sleepy Floyd 3/6/60
Thomas Foley 3/6/29
Stedman Graham 3/6/47
Alan Greenspan 3/6/26
Kiri Te Kanawa 3/6/44
Gabriel Garcia Marquez............. 3/6/28
Ed McMahon 3/6/23
JoAnna Miles 3/6/40
Ben Murphy 3/6/42
Hal Needham 3/6/31

Shaquille O'Neal 3/6/72
Rob Reiner 3/6/47
Willie Stargell 3/6/41
Mary Wilson 3/6/44

March 7
Willie "Flipper" Anderson 3/7/67
Anthony Armstrong-Jones 3/7/30
Joe Carter 3/7/60
King Curtis 3/7/34
Michael Eisner 3/7/42
Bert Ellis 3/7/64
Janet Guthrie 3/7/38
Franco Harris 3/7/50
John Heard 3/7/45
Ivan Lendl 3/7/60
Anna Magnani 3/7/09
Marice Revel 3/7/1875
Willard Scott 3/7/34
Lord Snowdon 3/7/30
Lynn Swann 3/7/52
Daniel Travanti 3/7/40
Peter Wolf 3/7/46

March 8
Dick Allen 3/8/42
Louise Beavers 3/8/02
Jim Bouton 3/8/39
Cyd Charisse 3/8/23
Susan Clark 3/8/44
Harold Cruse 3/8/16
Mickey Dolenz 3/8/45
Sam Jaffe 3/8/1893
Keith Jarrett 3/8/45
Sue Ann Langdon 3/8/36
Charley Pride 3/8/38
Aidan Quinn 3/8/59
Lynn Redgrave 3/8/43
Jim Rice 3/8/53
Carol Bayer Sager 3/8/47
Kenny Smith 3/8/65
Claire Trevor 3/8/09
Dain Turner 3/8/70
Buck Williams 3/8/60

March 9
Samuel Barber 3/9/10
Carl Betz 3/9/20
Brain Bosworth 3/9/65
Fernando Bujones 3/9/55
Bert Campaneris 3/9/42
Fred Clark 3/9/14
Faith Daniels 3/9/57
Bobby Fischer 3/9/43
Wil Geer 3/9/02
David Gergen 3/9/42
Charles Gibson 3/9/43
Mickey Gilley 3/9/36
Marty Ingels 3/9/36
Raul Julia 3/9/40
Michael Kinsley 3/9/51
Emanuel Lewis 3/9/71
Jeffrey Osbourne 3/9/48
Benito Santiago 3/9/65
Keely Smith 3/9/32
Mickey Spillane 3/9/18
Danny Sullivan 3/9/50
Trish Van Devere 3/9/45
Joyce Van Patten 3/9/34
Amerigo Vespucci 3/9/1451

March 10
Warner Anderson 3/10/11
Bix Beiderbecke 3/10/03
Heywood Hale Broun 3/10/18
Peter Deanda 3/10/38
Prince Edward 3/10/64
Barry Fitzgerald 3/10/1888
Mitch Gaylord 3/10/61
Bob Green 3/10/47
Jasmin Guy 3/10/64
Katharine Houghton 3/10/45
Cec Linder 3/10/21
Pamela Mason 3/10/22
Chuck Norris 3/10/40
David Rabe 3/10/40
Sharon Stone 3/10/58
Dean Torrence 3/10/41
Shannon Tweed 3/10/57

Jim Valvano 3/10/46
Raoul Walsh 3/10/1887
Andre Waters 3/10/62
Rod Woodson 3/10/65

March 11
Ralph Abernathy 3/11/26
Douglas Adams 3/11/52
Sam Donaldson 3/11/34
Ralph Waldo Ellison 3/11/14
Dorothy Gish 3/11/1898
Bobby McFerrin 3/11/50
Rupert Murdoch 3/11/31
Antonin Scalia 3/11/36
Lawrence Welk 3/11/03
Jerry Zucker 3/11/40

March 12
Edward Albee 3/12/28
Raul Alfonsin 3/12/27
Barbara Feldon 3/12/41
Marlon Jackson 3/12/57
Al Jarreau 3/12/40
Paul Kantner 3/12/42
Jack Kerouac 3/12/22
Lane Kirkland 3/12/22
Gordon MacRae 3/12/21
Evan Mecham 3/12/24
Liza Minnelli 3/12/46
Scoey Mitchell 3/12/30
Mark Moseley 3/12/48
Dale Murphy 3/12/56
Walter Schirra 3/12/23
Daryl Strawberry 3/12/62
James Taylor 3/12/48
Andrew Young 3/12/32
Mary Alice Williams 3/12/49

March 13
Walter Annenberg 3/13/08
Andy Bean 3/13/53
William Casey 3/13/13
Wil Clark 3/13/64
Adam Clayton 3/13/60

Dana Delany 3/13/56
Rosalind Elias 3/13/31
Juan Gris 3/13/1887
L. Ron Hubbard 3/13/11
Sammy Kaye 3/13/13
Charles Krauthammer 3/13/50
Madalyn Murray O'Hair 3/13/19
Caryl Phillips 3/13/58
Deborah Raffin 3/13/54
Neil Sedaka 3/13/39
Dan "Big Daddy" Wilkinson ... 3/13/73

March 14
Prince Albert 3/14/58
Diane Arbus 3/14/23
Frank Borman 3/14/28
Les Brown 3/14/12
Michael Caine 3/14/33
Eugene A. Cernan 3/14/34
Billy Crystal 3/14/47
Albert Einstein 3/14/1879
Horton Foote 3/14/16
William Clay Ford 3/14/25
Maxim Gorky 3/14/1868
Larry Johnson 3/14/69
Casey Jones 3/14/1864
Quincy Jones 3/14/33
Steven Kanaly 3/14/46
Hank Ketcham 3/14/20
Dennis Patrick 3/14/18
Kirby Puckett 3/14/61
Sloane Shelton 3/14/34
Rita Tushingham 3/14/42
Wes Unseld 3/14/46
Adrian Zmed 3/14/54

March 15
Harold Bains 3/15/59
Alan Bean 3/15/32
Bobby Bonds 3/15/46
George Brent 3/15/04
MacDonald Carey 3/15/14
Ry Cooder 3/15/47
Steve Coy 3/15/62

Terry Cummings 3/15/61
Terence Trent D'Arby 3/15/62
Fabio 3/15/61
Ruth Bader Ginsburg 3/15/33
Judd Hirsch 3/15/35
Lightnin Hopkins 3/15/07
Andrew Jackson 3/15/1767
Harry James 3/15/16
Mike Love 3/15/41
Ted Marchibroda 3/15/31
John Osborne 3/15/07
Park Overall 3/15/57
Federico Pena 3/15/47
Sabu 3/15/24
Dee Snider 3/15/55
Sly Stone 3/15/44
Jimmy Swaggart 3/15/35
Lawrence Tierney 3/15/19
Norm Van Brocklin 3/15/26
Lew Wasserman 3/15/13

March 16
Bernardo Bertolucci 3/16/40
Erik Estrada 3/16/49
Tommy Flanagan 3/16/30
Alice Hoffman 3/16/52
Jerry Lewis 3/16/26
Leo McKern 3/16/20
Daniel Moynihan 3/16/27
Conrad Nagel 3/16/1897
Kate Nelligan 3/16/51
Ozzie Newson 3/16/56
Patricia Nixon 3/16/12
Rodney Peete 3/16/66
Robert Rossen 3/16/08
Nancy Wilson (of Heart) 3/16/54

March 17
Danny Ainge 3/17/59
Sam Bowie 3/17/61
Frank Buck 3/17/1884
Nat "King" Cole 3/17/19
Lesley-Anne Down 3/17/54
Patrick Duffy 3/17/49

Cito Gaston 3/17/44
Eunice Gayson 3/17/31
Paul Horn 3/17/30
Shemp Howard 3/17/00
Bobby Jones 3/17/02
Penelope Lively 3/17/33
Rob Lowe 3/17/64
Mercedes McCambride 3/17/18
Rudolf Nureyev 3/17/38
Kurt Russell 3/17/51
Bayard Rustin 3/17/10
John Sebastian 3/17/44
Monique Van Vooren 3/17/33

March 18
Bonnie Blair 3/18/64
Smiley Burnette 3/18/11
John Caldwell Calhoun 3/18/1782
Irene Cara 3/18/59
Neville Chamberlain 3/18/1869
Grover Cleveland 3/18/1837
Richard Condon 3/18/15
W. F. deKlerk 3/18/36
Rudoph Diesel 3/18/1858
Kevin Dobson 3/18/44
Robert Donat 3/18/05
Brad Dourif 3/18/50
Capt. William Driver 3/18/1803
Peter Graves 3/18/26
Edward Everett Horton 3/18/1886
Mollie Parnis 3/18/05
Wilson Pickett 3/18/41
George Plimpton 3/18/27
Nikolai Rimsky-Korsakov ... 3/18/1844
Ingemar Stenmark 3/18/56
John Updike 3/18/32
Vanessa Williams 3/18/63

March 19
Ursula Andress 3/19/36
William Jennings Bryan 3/19/1860
Glenn Close 3/19/47
Ornette Coleman 3/19/30
Sergei Diaghiler 3/19/1872

Wyatt Earp 3/19/1849
Adolf Eichmann 3/19/06
Louis Hayward 3/19/09
Lynda Bird Johnson 3/19/44
Moms Mabley 3/19/1894
Patrick McGoohan 3/19/28
Phyllis Newman 3/19/35
Philip Roth 3/19/33
Brent Scowcroft 3/19/25
Sirhan Sirhan 3/19/44
John Sirica 3/19/04
Albert Speer 3/19/05
Kent Smith 3/19/07
Irving Wallace 3/19/16
Earl Warren 3/19/1891
Bruce Willis 3/19/55

March 20

Philip Abbott 3/20/24
Mookie Blaylock 3/20/67
Edgar Buchanan 3/20/03
Wendell Corey 3/20/14
Larry Elgart 3/20/22
Ray Goulding 3/20/22
Holly Hunter 3/20/58
William Hurt 3/20/50
Henrik Ibsen 3/20/1828
Jack Kruschen 3/20/22
Spike Lee 3/20/57
Hal Linden 3/20/31
Lauritz Melchior 3/20/1890
Nicole Miller 3/20/51
Brian Mulroney 3/20/39
Ozzie Nelson 3/20/06
Bobby Orr 3/20/48
Michael Redgrave 3/20/08
Jerry Reed 3/20/37
Carl Reiner 3/20/22
Pat Riley 3/20/45
Mr. (Fred) Roger 3/20/28
Theresa Russell 3/20/57
Benno Schmidt, Jr. 3/20/42
B.F. Skinner 3/20/04

March 21

Johann Sebastian Bach 3/21/1685
John Boylan 3/21/41
Matthew Broderick 3/21/62
Peter Brook 3/21/25
Edgar Buchanan 3/21/03
James Coco 3/21/29
Timothy Dalton 3/21/46
Francoise Dorleac 3/21/42
Tom Flores 3/21/37
Al Freeman, Jr. 3/21/34
Benito Juarez 3/21/1806
Mort Lindsey 3/21/23
M.P. Mussorgsky 3/21/1839
Gary Oldman 3/21/58
Kathleen Widdoes 3/21/39
Florenz Ziegfeld 3/21/1867

March 22

George Benson 3/22/43
Derek Bok 3/22/30
Shawn Bradley 3/22/72
May Britt 3/22/33
Don Chaney 3/22/46
Bob Costas 3/22/52
Orrin Hatch 3/22/34
Werner Klemperer 3/22/20
Karl Malden 3/22/13
Marcel Marceau 3/22/23
"Chico" Marx 3/22/1891
Giulietta Masina 3/22/21
J.P. McCarthy 3/22/34
Stephanie Mills 3/22/57
Matthew Modine 3/22/59
Nicholas Monsarrat 3/22/10
Al Neuharth 3/22/24
Lena Olin 3/22/55
Pat Robertson 3/22/30
Bud Sagendorf 3/22/15
William Shatner 3/22/31
Stephen Sondheim 3/22/30
Andrew Lloyd Webber 3/22/48

March 23

Marty Allen 3/23/22
Roger Bannister 3/23/29
Craig Breedlove 3/23/37
Joan Crawford 3/23/08
Hazel Dawn 3/23/1898
Erich Fromm 3/23/00
Maynard Jackson 3/23/38
Chaka Khan 3/23/53
Jason Kidd 3/23/73
Akira Kurosawa 3/23/10
Moses Malone 3/23/55
Ric Ocasek 3/23/49
Amanda Plummer 3/23/57
Wernher Von Braun 3/23/12
David Watkins 3/23/25

March 24

Wilson Alvarez 3/24/70
Fatty Arbuckle 3/24/1887
Clyde Barrow 3/24/09
Freddie Bartholomew 3/24/24
Pat Bradley 3/24/51
Vanessa Brown 3/24/28
Robert Carradine 3/24/54
Lucia Chase 3/24/07
Richard Conte 3/24/14
Thomas Dewey 3/24/02
Norman Fell 3/24/25
Lawrence Ferlinghetti 3/24/19
Donald Hamilton 3/24/16
Harry Houdini 3/24/1887
Byron Janis 3/24/28
Bob Mackie 3/24/40
Steve McQueen 3/24/30
Andrew Mellon 3/24/1855
Malcolm Muggeridge 3/24/03
Gene Nelson 3/24/20
Donna Pescow 3/24/54
Wilhelm Reich 3/24/1897
Kathy Rinald 3/24/67
John Rock 3/24/1890
William Smith 3/24/33

March 25

Hoyt Axton 3/25/35
Bonnie Bedelia 3/25/48
Ed Begley 3/25/01
Gutzon Borglum 3/25/1867
Anita Bryant 3/25/40
Howard Cosell 3/25/20
Eileen Otte Ford 3/25/22
Aretha Franklin 3/25/42
Paul Michael Glaser 3/25/42
Mary Gross 3/25/53
Elton John 3/25/47
David Lean 3/25/08
James Lovell 3/25/23
Tom Monaghan 3/25/37
Flannery O'Connor 3/25/25
Sarah Jessica Parker 3/25/65
Simone Signoret 3/25/21
Gloria Steinem 3/25/35
Debi Thomas 3/25/67
Arturo Toscanini 3/25/1867
Jean Vilar 3/25/12
Roger Wilkins 3/25/32

March 26

Marcus Allen 3/26/60
Phillip Richard Allen 3/26/39
Alan Arkin 3/26/34
Pierre Boulez 3/26/25
James Caan 3/26/39
Bob Elliott 3/26/23
Robert Frost 3/26/1874
Sterling Hayden 3/26/16
Duncan Hines 3/26/1880
Erica Jong 3/26/42
Vicki Lawrence 3/26/49
Conde Nast 3/26/1874
Leonard Nimoy 3/26/31
Sandra Day O'Connor 3/26/30
Leeza Gibbons 3/26/57
Teddy Pendergrass 3/26/50
Diana Ross 3/26/44
Martin Short 3/26/50
Curtis Sliwa 3/26/54

Edward Sovel 3/26/29
John Stockton 3/26/62
Steven Tyler 3/26/48
William Westmoreland 3/26/14
Tennessee Williams 3/26/11
Bob Woodward 3/26/43

March 27
Mariah Carey 3/27/70
Randall Cunningham 3/27/63
Maria Ewing 3/27/50
Joan Fleming 3/27/08
Patty Smith Hill 3/27/1868
David Jannsen 3/27/31
Jerry Lacy 3/27/36
Snooky Lanson 3/27/19
Anthony Lewis 3/27/27
Arthur Mitchell 3/27/34
Pee Wee Russell 3/27/06
Maria Schneider 3/27/52
Budd Schulberg 3/27/14
Edward Steichen 3/27/1879
Gloria Swanson 3/27/1899
Quentin Tarantino 3/27/63
Cyrus Vance 3/27/17
Miles Van de Rohe 3/27/1899
Sarah Vaughan 3/27/24
Caleb Yarborough 3/27/40
Michael York 3/27/42

March 28
Nelson Algrew 3/28/09
Bob Allen 3/28/06
Rick Barry 3/28/44
Pandro Berman 3/28/05
Dirk Bogarde 3/28/21
Zbigniew Brzezinski 3/28/28
August Busch, Jr. 3/28/1899
Conchata Ferrell 3/28/43
Ken Howard 3/28/44
Irving Lazar 3/28/07
Frank Lovejoy 3/28/14
Reba McEntire 3/28/55
Ed Muskie 3/28/14

Dennis O'Keefe 3/28/10
Marlin Perkins 3/28/05
Frederick Pabst 3/28/1836
Ken Howard 3/28/44
Raphael 3/28/1483
Byron Scott 3/28/61
Rudolph Serkin 3/28/03
Jerry Sloan 3/28/42
John Tyler 3/28/1790
Paul Whiteman 3/28/1891
Dianne Wiest 3/28/48

March 29
Pearl Bailey 3/29/18
Warner Baxter 3/29/1891
Earl Campbell 3/29/55
Jennifer Capriati 3/29/76
Billy Carter 3/29/37
Bud Cort 3/29/51
Phil Foster 3/29/14
Walt Frazier 3/29/45
Eileen Heckart 3/29/19
Derek Humphrey 3/29/30
Eric Idle 3/29/43
Karen Kain 3/29/51
Bobby Kimbal 3/29/47
Jay Livingston 3/29/15
John Major 3/29/43
Eugene McCarthy 3/29/16
Reba McIntire 3/29/55
Denny McLain 3/29/44
John McLaughlin 3/29/27
Arthur O'Connell 3/29/08
Oscar 3/29/1859
Karen Ann Quinlan 3/29/54
Kurt Thomas 3/29/56
Vangelis 3/29/43
Sam Walton 3/29/18
Cy Young 3/29/1867

March 30
John Astin 3/30/30
Warren Beatty 3/30/37
Turhan Bey 3/30/20

McGeorge Bundy 3/30/19
Eric Clapton 3/30/45
Richard Dysart 3/30/29
Bob Evans.................................. 3/30/18
Hammer 3/30/63
Frankie Laine 3/30/13
Peter Marshall 3/30/30
Sean O'Casey 3/30/1880
Paul Reiser 3/30/57
Vincent Van Gogh 3/30/1853

March 31

Herb Alpert............................... 3/31/35
Leo Buscaglia 3/31/25
Richard Chamberlain 3/31/35
Cesar Chavez............................ 3/31/27
Liz Claiborne 3/31/29
William Daniels........................ 3/31/27
John Fowles 3/31/26
Barney Frank 3/31/40
Lefty Frizzell............................. 3/31/28
Nikolai Gogol 3/31/1809
Albert Gore 3/31/48
Joseph Hayden 3/31/1732
Glenne Aimee Headly.............. 3/31/58
Gordon Howe............................ 3/31/28
John Jakes................................. 3/31/32
Jack Johnson 3/31/1878
Shirley Jones 3/31/34
Gabe Kaplan 3/31/45
Richard Kiley 3/31/22
Patrick Leahy 3/31/40
John D. Loudermilk 3/31/34
Henry Morgan 3/31/15
Rhea Perlman 3/31/46
Marge Piercy............................ 3/31/36
J.R. Reid 3/31/68
Steve Smith 3/31/69
Brandon Stoddard 3/31/37
Christopher Walken 3/31/43
James Yaffe 3/31/27

April 1

George Baker 4/1/31

Wallace Beery 4/1/1886
Lon Chaney............................... 4/1/1883
Hans Conreid 4/1/15
Eddie Duchin............................ 4/1/09
Kevin Duckworth 4/1/64
George Grizzard 4/1/28
Alberta Hunter 4/1/1897
Robert Isley 4/1/39
Mark Jackson 4/1/65
Ali MacGraw 4/1/38
Magdalena Maleeva 4/1/75
Abraham Maslow 4/1/08
Toshiro Mifune.......................... 4/1/20
Nita Naldi 4/1/1899
Annette O'Toole 4/1/53
Jane Powell 4/1/28
Sergei Rachmaninoff 4/1/1873
Debbie Reynolds 4/1/32
Edmond Rostand 4/1/1868
Bo Schembechler 4/1/29
Gill Scott-Heron 4/1/49
Laurette Taylor...................... 4/1/1887

April 2

Sharon Acker 4/2/35
Frederic Bartholdi 4/2/1834
Dana Carvey 4/2/55
Charlemagne .... 4/2/742 AD
Hans Christian Andersen 4/2/1805
Billy Dean................................. 4/2/62
Buddy Ebsen.............................. 4/2/08
Rita Gam 4/2/28
Marvin Gaye 4/2/39
Sir Alec Guiness 4/2/14
Emmylou Harris 4/2/48
Linda Hunt 4/2/45
Anthony Lake............................ 4/2/63
Camille Paglia 4/2/47
Ron Palillo................................ 4/2/54
Pamela Reed 4/2/49
Leon Russell.............................. 4/2/41
Debralee Scott........................... 4/2/53
Don Sutton 4/2/45
Kenneth Tynan.......................... 4/2/27

Jack Webb 4/2/20

Emile Zola 4/2/1840

April 3

Alec Baldwin 4/3/58

Jan Berry 4/3/43

Marlon Brando 4/3/24

Lawton Chiles 4/3/30

Iron Eyes Cody 4/3/15

Doris Day 4/3/24

Allan Dwan 4/3/1885

Jennie Garth 4/3/72

Jane Goodall 4/3/34

Virgil Grissom 4/3/26

George Jessel 4/3/1898

Henry Luce 4/3/1898

Marsha Mason 4/3/42

Eddie Murphy 4/3/61

Wayne Newton 4/3/42

Tony Orlando 4/3/44

David Hyde Pierce 4/3/59

Jan Sterling 4/3/23

Boss Tweed 4/3/1823

Miyoshi Umeki 4/3/29

Dooley Wilson 4/3/1894

April 4

Maya Angelou 4/4/28

Elmer Bernstein 4/4/22

Bijan 4/4/40

Robert Downey, Jr. 4/4/65

Jim Fregosi 4/4/42

A. Bartlett Giamatti 4/4/38

Gil Hodges 4/4/24

Kitty Kelley 4/4/42

Frances Langford 4/4/14

Richard Lugar 4/4/32

William Manchester 4/4/22

Hugh Masekela 4/4/39

Nancy McKeon 4/4/66

Arthur Murray 4/4/1895

Craig T. Nelson 4/4/46

Anthony Perkins 4/4/32

Eric Rohmer 4/4/22

John Cameron Swayze 4/4/06

Muddy Waters 4/4/15

Jerome Weidman 4/4/13

April 5

Albert "Cubby" Broccoli 4/5/09

Roger Corman 4/5/26

Betty Davis 4/5/08

Melvin Douglas 4/5/01

Max Gail 4/5/43

Frank Gorshin 4/5/34

Arthur Hailey 4/5/20

Arthur Haley 4/5/20

Thomas Hobbes 4/5/1588

Walter Huston 4/5/1884

Christine Lahti 4/5/50

Michael Moriarty 4/5/42

Gerry Mulligan 4/5/27

Gregory Peck 4/5/16

Colin Powell 4/5/37

Gale Storm 4/5/22

Spencer Tracy 4/5/00

Stanley Turrentine 4/5/34

Booker T. Washington 4/5/1856

April 6

Butch Cassidy 4/6/1867

Merle Haggard 4/6/37

Marilu Henner 4/6/53

Jerry Krause 4/6/39

Barry Levinson 4/6/32

Janet Lynn 4/6/53

Bronislaw Malinowski 4/6/1884

Michell Phillips 4/6/44

Andre Previn 4/6/29

John Ratzenberger 4/6/47

George Reeves 4/6/14

John Sculley 4/6/39

Sterling Sharpe 4/6/65

Lowell Thomas 4/6/1892

Billy Dee Williams 4/6/37

April 7

Bobby Bare 4/7/35

Donald Barthelme	4/7/31
Jerry Brown	4/7/38
Hodding Carter III	4/7/35
Irene Castle	4/7/1893
Francis Coppola	4/7/39
Christopher Darden	4/7/56
Tony Dorsett	4/7/54
James "Buster" Douglas	4/7/60
Percy Faith	4/7/08
David Frost	4/7/39
James Garner	4/7/28
Billie Holiday	4/7/15
Freddie Hubbard	4/7/38
Preston Jones	4/7/36
W.K. Kellogg	4/7/1860
John Oates	4/7/49
Alan Pakula	4/7/28
Julia Miller Phillips	4/7/44
Wayne Rogers	4/7/33
Ricky Watters	4/7/69
Bert Wheeler	4/7/1895
Walter Winchell	4/7/1897

April 8

Michael Bennett	4/8/43
Jacques Brel	4/8/29
Franco Carelli	4/8/23
Gary Carter	4/8/54
Mark Clayton	4/8/61
Franco Corelli	4/8/23
Betty Ford	4/8/18
John Gavin	4/8/32
Shecky Greene	4/8/26
John Havlicek	4/8/40
Sonja Henie	4/8/12
Steve Howe	4/8/47
Leon Huff	4/8/42
Robert L. Johnson	4/8/46
Barbara Kingsolver	4/8/55
Julian Lennon	4/8/63
Carmen McRae	4/8/22
Edward Mulhare	4/8/47
Mary Pickford	4/8/1894
Terry Porter	4/8/63

John Schneider	4/8/54
Ian Smith	4/8/19

April 9

Severiano Ballesteras	4/9/57
Jean-Paul Belmondo	4/9/33
Ward Bond	4/9/04
William J. Fullbright	4/9/05
Hugh Hefner	4/9/26
Hal Ketchum	4/9/53
Bo Kimble	4/9/66
Michael Learned	4/9/39
Nikolai Lenin	4/9/1870
James McDonnell	4/9/1899
Carl Perkins	4/9/32
Paulina Porizkova	4/9/65
Keshia Knight Pulliam	4/9/79
Dennis Quaid	4/9/54
Paul Robeson	4/9/1898

April 10

George Arliss	4/10/1868
Chuck Connors	4/10/21
Ken Griffey, Sr.	4/10/50
David Halberstam	4/10/34
John Daniel Hertz	4/10/1879
Clare Boothe Luce	4/10/03
John Madden	4/10/36
Tim McCoy	4/10/1891
Don Meredith	4/10/38
Harry Morgan	4/10/15
Joseph Pulitzer	4/10/1847
Steven Seagal	4/10/52
Terry Teagle	4/10/60
Paul Theroux	4/10/41
Cathy Turner	4/10/62
Max Von Sydow	4/10/29
Lew Wallace	4/10/1827
Sheb Wooley	4/10/21

April 11

Dean Acheson	4/11/1893
Nicholas Brady	4/11/30
Tony Brown	4/11/33

Oleg Cassini 4/11/13
Ellen Goodman 4/11/41
Joel Grey 4/11/32
Charles Evans Hughes 4/11/1862
Bill Irwin 4/11/50
Ethel Kennedy 4/11/28
Howard Koch 4/11/16
Louis Lasser 4/11/39
John Milius 4/11/44
Peter Riegert 4/11/47
Leo Rosten 4/11/08
Bert Saberhagen 4/11/64
David Westheimer 4/11/17
Andrew J. Wiles 4/11/53

April 12
Alan Ayckbourn 4/12/39
Montserrat Caballe 4/12/33
David Cassidy 4/12/50
Shannen Doherty 4/12/71
Gerald Early 4/12/52
Andy Garcia 4/12/56
Vince Gill 4/12/57
Lionel Hampton 4/12/13
Herbie Hancock 4/12/40
David Letterman 4/12/47
Charles Ludlam 4/12/43
Charles Mann 4/12/61
Ann Miller 4/12/23
Ed O'Neill 4/12/46
Lily Pons 4/12/04
Tiny Tim 4/12/22
Scott Turow 4/12/49
Jane Withers 4/12/26
Elaine Zayak 4/12/58

April 13
Samuel Beckett 4/13/06
Mari Blanchard 4/13/27
Peabo Bryson 4/13/51
Ben Nighthorse Campbell 4/13/33
Bill Conti 4/13/42
Stanley Donen 4/13/24
Edward Fox 4/13/37

Rev. Al Green 4/13/46
Thomas Jefferson 4/13/1743
Gary Kasparov 4/13/63
Howard Keel 4/13/19
Davis Love III 4/13/64
Catherine de Medici 4/13/1519
Madalyn Murray O'Hair 3/13/19
Ron Perlman 4/13/50
Herman Raucher 4/13/28
Ricky Schroeder 4/13/70
Harold Stassen 4/13/07
Erich Von Daniken 4/13/35
Lyle Waggoner 4/13/35
Eudora Welty 4/13/09
Lanford Wilson 4/13/37

April 14
Jeffrey Archer 4/14/40
Julie Christie 4/14/40
Bradford Dillman 4/14/30
Sir John Gielgud 4/14/04
Anthony Michael Hall 4/14/68
David Justice 4/14/66
Loretta Lynn 4/14/35
Greg Maddux 4/14/66
Pete Rose 4/14/41
Joseph Ruskin 4/14/24
Frank Serpico 4/14/36
Rod Steiger 4/14/25

April 15
Michael Ansara 4/15/22
Evelyn Ashford 4/15/57
Thomas Hart Benton 4/15/1889
Linda Bloodworth-Thomason . 4/15/47
Claudia Cardinale 4/15/38
Roy Clark 4/15/33
Michael Cooper 4/15/56
Leonardo de Vinci 4/15/1452
Dave Edmunds 4/15/44
Heloise 4/15/51
Henry James 4/15/1843
Harvey Lembeck 4/15/23
Elizabeth Montgomery 4/15/33

Wallace Reid 4/15/1891
Bessie Smith 4/15/1894
Emma Thompson 4/15/59
Harold Washington 4/15/22

April 16

Kareem Abdul-Jabbar 4/16/47
Edie Adams 4/16/29
Polly Adler 4/16/00
Kingsley Amis 4/16/22
Ellen Barkin 4/16/55
Charlie Chaplin 4/16/1889
Merce Cunningham 4/16/19
Fifi D'Orsay 4/16/04
Dennis Russell Davies 4/16/44
Johnny Grier 4/16/47
Luke Haas 4/16/76
John Hodiak 4/16/14
Henry Mancini 4/16/24
Spike Milligan 4/16/18
Barry Nelson 4/16/20
Peter Mark Richman 4/16/27
Dusty Springfield 4/16/39
Robert Stigwood 4/16/34
Peter Ustinov 4/16/21
Bobby Vinton 4/16/35
Wilbur Wright 4/16/1867

April 17

Lindsay Anderson 4/17/23
Clarence Darrow 4/17/1857
"Boomer" Esiason 4/17/61
Gen. Joe Foss 4/17/15
Marquis Grissom 4/17/67
Jan Hammer 4/17/48
William Holden 4/17/18
Olivia Hussey 4/17/51
Nikita Khrushchev 4/17/1894
Don Kirshner 4/17/34
Arthur Lakes 4/17/05
J.P. Morgan 4/17/1837
Harry Reasoner 4/17/23
Anne Shirley 4/17/18
Thornton Wilder 4/17/1897

April 18

Wendy Barrie 4/18/10
Barbara Hale 4/18/22
Huntington Hartford 4/18/11
Jim "Catfish" Hunter 4/18/46
Deacon Jones 4/18/34
Wilber Marshall 4/18/62
Hayley Mills 4/18/46
Rick Moranis 4/18/54
Conan O'Brien 4/18/63
Clive Revill 4/18/30
Eric Roberts 4/18/56
Miklos Rozsa 4/18/07
Dick Sargent 4/18/19
Leopold Stokowski 4/18/1882
James Woods 4/18/47

April 19

Paula Abdul 4/19/62
Don Adams 4/19/27
Fernando Botero 4/19/32
Tim Curry 4/19/46
Elinor Donahue 4/19/37
Frank Fontaine 4/19/20
Keith Jackson (football) 4/19/65
Jayne Mansfield 4/19/32
Dudley Moore 4/19/35
Eliot Ness 4/19/03
Hugh O'Brian 4/19/30
Paloma Picasso 4/19/49
Alan Price 4/19/42
Constance Talmadge 4/19/00
Al Unser, Jr. 4/19/62
Frank Viola 4/19/60

April 20

Bruce Cabot 4/20/04
Joseph Camp 4/20/39
Daniel Day-Lewis 4/20/58
Harvey Firestone 4/20/1898
Nina Foch 4/20/24
Adolf Hitler 4/20/1889
Jessica Lange 4/20/49
Harold Lloyd 4/20/1893

Don Mattingly 4/20/61
Joan Miro 4/20/1893
Ryan O'Neal 4/20/41
Tito Puente 4/20/23
Gregory Ratoff 4/20/1893
Justice John Stevens 4/20/20
Luther Vandross 4/20/51

April 21
David Boren 4/21/41
Joseph Bottoms 4/22/54
Charlotte Bronte 4/21/1816
Don Cornell 4/21/19
Tony Danza 4/21/51
Queen Elizabeth II 4/21/26
Gary Grant 4/21/65
Charles Grodin 4/21/35
Patti Lupone 4/21/49
Andie MacDowell 4/21/58
Silvava Mangano 4/21/30
Elaine May 4/21/32
Rollo May 4/21/09
Daniel Melnick 4/21/32
Iggy Pop 4/21/47
Anthony Quinn 4/21/16

April 22
Eddie Albert 4/22/08
Byron Allen 4/22/62
Glen Campbell 4/22/38
Peter Frampton 4/22/50
Spencer Haywood 4/22/49
Yehudi Menuhin 4/22/16
Jason Miller 4/22/39
Charles Mingus 4/22/22
Jack Nicholson 4/22/37
Aaron Spelling 4/22/25
John Waters 4/22/46

April 23
Valerie Bertinelli 4/23/60
David Birney 4/23/40
Janet Blair 4/23/21
Sandra Dee 4/23/42

Joyce Dewitt 4/23/49
J.P. Donleavy 4/23/26
Halston 4/23/32
Jan Hooks 4/23/57
Lee Majors 4/23/40
Vladimir Nabokov 4/23/1899
Ronald Neame 4/23/11
Roy Orbison 4/23/36
Sergei Prokofiev 4/23/1891
Duncan Renaldo 4/23/04
William Shakespeare 4/23/1564
Warren Spahn 4/23/21
Shirley Temple-Black 4/23/28
Herve Villachaize 4/23/43

April 24
Eric Bogosian 4/24/53
William Castle 4/24/14
Richard Daley 4/24/42
William Dekooning 4/24/04
Sue Grafton 4/24/40
Leslie Howard 4/24/1893
Jill Ireland 4/24/36
Stanley Kauffman 4/24/16
Jack E. Leonard 4/24/11
Shirley MacLaine 4/24/34
Richard Sterban 4/24/43
Barbra Streisand 4/24/42
Anthony Trollope 4/24/1815
Robert Penn Warren 4/24/05

April 25
William Brennan, Jr. 4/25/06
Dave Corzine 4/25/56
Ella Fitzgerald 4/25/18
Travis Fryman 4/25/69
Melissa Hayden 4/25/28
Albert King 4/25/23
Meadowlark Lemon 4/25/32
Paul Mazursky 4/25/30
Edward R. Murrow 4/25/08
Al Pacino 4/25/40
Tony Phillips 4/25/59
Talia Shire 4/25/46

Randall Terry 4/25/59

April 26
Carol Burnett 4/26/36
Michael Damian 4/26/62
Duane Eddy 4/26/38
Rudolf Hess 4/26/1894
Bambi Linn.............................. 4/26/26
Anita Loos 4/26/1893
Bernard Malamud.................... 4/26/16
I.M. Pei.................................... 4/26/17
Charlotte Rae 4/26/26
Bobby Rydell 4/26/42
T-Boz....................................... 4/26/70
Roger Taylor 4/26/60
Morris West 4/26/16
Gary Wright............................. 4/26/43

April 27
Anouk Aimee 4/27/34
Arthur Burns 4/27/04
Sandy Dennis........................... 4/27/37
Sheena Easton.......................... 4/27/59
George Gervin 4/27/52
Ulysses S. Grant 4/27/1822
Coretta Scott-King 4/27/27
Jack Klugman 4/27/22
Chuck Knox 4/27/32
Walter Lantz 4/27/00
August Wilson 4/27/45

April 28
Ann-Margret............................ 4/28/41
Robert Anderson 4/28/17
James Baker III 4/28/30
Lionel Barrymore 4/28/1878
Blossom Dearie........................ 4/28/26
Rowland Evans, Jr. 4/28/21
Melissa Joan Hart..................... 4/28/76
Saddam Hussein 4/28/37
Carolyn Jones 4/28/33
Bruno Kirby 4/28/48
Harper Lee 4/28/26
Jay Leno................................... 4/28/50

Madge Sinclair......................... 4/28/40
Marcia Strassman..................... 4/28/48
Sidney Toler............................ 4/28/1874
Too Short.................................. 4/28/66

April 29
Andre Agassi 4/29/70
Duane Allen 4/29/43
George Allen............................ 4/29/22
Keith Baxter 4/29/35
Sir Thomas Beecham 4/29/1879
Richard Carlson 4/29/12
Dale Earnhardt 4/29/40
Duke Ellington 4/29/1899
Celeste Ewell 4/29/19
Tom Ewell 4/29/09
William Randolph Hearst.... 4/29/1863
Emperor Hirohito 4/29/01
Celeste Holm 4/29/19
Rod McKuen............................. 4/29/33
Zubin Mehta 4/29/36
Johnny Miller........................... 4/29/47
Kate Mulgrew 4/29/55
Michelle Pfeiffer 4/29/58
Rafael Sabatini 4/29/1875
George Schulz........................... 4/29/25
Jerry Seinfeld 4/29/54
Robert Tisch 4/29/26
Fred Zinnemann 4/29/07

April 30
Eve Arden 4/30/12
John Bagley 4/30/60
Corinne Calvet 4/30/25
Jill Clayburgh 4/30/44
Sheldon Harnick 4/30/24
Johnny Horton.......................... 4/30/27
Perry King 4/30/48
Cloris Leachman 4/30/26
Franz Lehar 4/30/1870
Willie Nelson 4/30/33
Robert Shaw 4/30/16
Isiah Thomas 4/30/61
Al Toon 4/30/63

Burt Young 4/30/40
Ian Ziering 4/30/64

May 1

Doug Barr 5/1/49
Scott Carpenter 5/1/25
Steve Cauthen 5/1/60
Gary Clark 5/1/62
Gen. Mark Clark 5/1/1896
Judy Collins 5/1/39
Johnny Colt 5/1/68
Rita Coolidge 5/1/45
Danielle Darrieux 5/1/17
Glen Ford 5/1/16
Joseph Heller 5/1/23
Chris Kelly 5/1/78
Billy Owens 5/1/69
Jack Paar 5/1/18
Max Robinson 5/1/39
Kate Smith 5/1/09
Terry Southern 5/1/24

May 2

Brian Aherne 5/2/02
Christine Baranski 5/2/52
Theodore Bikel 5/2/24
Roscoe Lee Browne 5/2/25
Vernon Castle 5/2/1887
Catherine the Great 5/2/1729
Bing Crosby 5/2/04
Larry Gatlin 5/2/49
Lesley Gore 5/2/46
Philippe Halsman 5/2/06
Lorenz Hart 5/2/1895
Bianca Jagger 5/2/45
John Neville 5/2/25
Dan O'Herlihy 5/2/19
Bernard Slade 5/2/30
Benjamin Spock 5/2/03
Baron Von Richthofen 5/2/1892

May 3

Mary Astor 5/3/06
Beulah Bondi 5/3/1892

James Brown 5/3/36
Betty Comden 5/3/15
Norman Corwin 5/3/10
Christopher Cross 5/3/51
Maynard Ferguson 5/3/28
Greg Gumbel 5/3/46
Doug Henning 5/3/47
Jeff Hornacek 5/3/63
Engelbert Humperdinck 5/3/36
William Inge 5/3/13
Lash La Rue 5/3/02
Joe Layton 5/3/31
Davey Lopes 5/3/45
Golda Meir 5/3/1898
Sugar Ray Robinson 5/3/21
Pete Seeger 5/3/19
Walter Slezak 5/3/02
Alida Valli 5/3/21
Frankie Valli 5/3/37

May 4

Nicholas Ashford 5/4/43
Howard DaSilva 5/4/09
Tyrone Davis 5/4/38
Keith Haring 5/4/58
Audrey Hepburn 5/4/29
Hilly Hicks 5/4/50
Jackie Jackson 5/4/51
Hosni Mubarak 5/4/28
Roberta Peters 5/4/30
Randy Travis 5/4/59
George Will 5/4/41

May 5

Nellie Bly 5/5/1867
Pat Carrol 5/5/27
Ann B. Davis 5/5/26
Alice Faye 5/5/15
Sigmund Freud 5/5/1856
Freeman Gosden 5/5/1899
Arthur Hailey 5/5/20
Soren Kierkegaard 5/5/1813
Bob Marley 5/5/45
Karl Marx 5/5/1818

Christopher Morley 5/5/1890
Michael Murphy 5/5/38
Michael Palin 5/5/43
Tyrone Power 5/5/14
Henryk Sienkiewicz 5/5/1846
Tammy Wynette 5/5/42
Tina Yothers 5/5/73
Bob Marley 5/5/45

May 6

Carmen Cavallaro 5/6/13
Mark Bryan 5/6/67
George Clooney 5/6/61
Stewart Granger 5/6/13
Ross Hunter 5/6/24
Willie Mays 5/6/31
Max Ophuls 5/6/02
Robert E. Peary 5/6/1856
Bob Seger 5/6/45
Toots Shor 5/6/05
Rudolph Valentino 5/6/1895
Orson Welles 5/6/15
Theodore White 5/6/15

May 7

Anne Baxter 5/7/23
Theresa Brewer 5/7/31
Robert Browning 5/7/1812
Joe Clark 5/7/39
Gary Cooper 5/7/01
Pete Domenici 5/7/32
Totie Fields 5/7/30
Ronnie Harmon 5/7/64
Gabby Hayes 5/7/1855
Janis Ian 5/7/50
Edwin Land 5/7/09
Traci Lords 5/7/68
Archibald MacLeish 5/7/1892
Darren McGavin 5/7/22
Marvin Mitchlson 5/7/28
Eva Peron 5/7/19
Carolyne Roehm 5/7/51
Jimmy Ruffin 5/7/39
Robin Strasser 5/7/45

Peter Ilyich Tchaikovsky 5/7/1840
Johnny Unitas 5/7/33

May 8

David Attenborough 5/8/26
Philip Bailey 5/8/51
Lex Barker 5/8/19
Saul Bass 5/8/20
Peter Benchley 5/8/40
Dennis DeConcini 5/8/37
Fernandel 5/8/02
Melissa Gilbert 5/8/64
Beth Henley 5/8/52
David Keith 5/8/54
Sonny Liston 5/8/32
Ronnie Lott 5/8/59
Carmen Mathews 5/8/18
Ricky Nelson 5/8/40
Thomas Pynchons 5/8/37
Don Rickles 5/8/26
Roberto Rossellini 5/8/06
Arnold Scaasi 5/8/31
Bishop Fulton Sheen 5/8/1895
Theodore Sorensen 5/8/28
Toni Tennille 5/8/43
Harry S. Truman 5/8/1884
Alex Van Halen 5/8/55
Edmund Wilson 5/8/1895

May 9

Pedro Armendariz 5/9/12
Richard Barthelmess 5/9/1895
Candice Bergen 5/9/46
James L. Brooks 5/9/40
John Brown 5/9/1800
Albert Finney 5/9/36
Richie Furay 5/9/44
Dave Gahan 5/9/62
Jose Ortega Gasset 5/9/1883
Pancho Gonzales 5/9/28
Tony Gwynn 5/9/60
Glenda Jackson 5/9/37
Billy Joel 5/9/49
Henry J. Kaiser 5/9/1882

John Mahaffey 5/9/48	Denver Pyle 5/11/20
Anne Sofiv Offer 5/9/55	Randy Quaid 5/11/50
Tommy Roe 5/9/42	Natasha Richardson 5/11/63
Hank Snow 5/9/14	Margaret Rutherford 5/11/1892
Mike Wallace 5/9/18	Mort Sahl 5/11/27
Steve Yzerman 5/9/65	Phil Silvers 5/11/12

May 10

Fred Astaire 5/10/1899	Mary Kay Ash 5/12/15
Bono 5/10/60	Burt Bacharach 5/12/29
John Wilkes Booth 5/10/1838	Yoga Berra 5/12/25
T. Berry Brazelton 5/10/18	Bruce Boxleitner 5/12/51
Mark David Chapman 5/10/55	George Carlin 5/12/37
Teri Copley 5/10/61	Lindsay Crouse 5/12/48
Wayne Dyer 5/10/40	Guillermo Endara 5/12/36
Linda Evangelista 5/10/65	Emilio Estevez 5/12/62
Francoise Fabian 5/10/35	Kim Fields 5/12/69
Judith Jamison 5/10/34	Susan Hampshire 5/12/42
Arthur L. Kopit 5/10/37	Wilfred Hyde-White 5/12/03
Phil Mahre 5/10/57	Florence Nightingale 5/12/1820
Steve Hahre 5/10/57	Millie Perkins 5/12/40
Donovan Leitch 5/10/46	Julius Rosenberg 5/12/18
Dave Mason 5/10/46	Howard K. Smith 5/12/14
Chris Novoselic 5/10/65	Tom Snyder 5/12/36
Merlene Ottey 5/10/60	Lou Whitaker 5/12/57
Gary Owens 5/10/35	Steve Winwood 5/12/48
Rony Seikaly 5/10/65	
David O. Selznick 5/10/02	### May 13
Nicole Brown Simpson 5/10/59	Franklin Ajaye 5/13/49
Pat Summerall 5/10/31	Beatrice Arthur 5/13/26
Young MC 5/10/67	Clive Barnes 5/13/27
Nancy Walker 5/10/22	Daphne DuMaurier 5/13//07
	Harvey Keitel 5/13/39
### May 11	Joe Louis 5/13/14
Irving Berlin 5/11/1888	Herbert Ross 5/13/27
Foster Brooks 5/11/12	Richie Valens 5/13/41
Salvador Dali 5/11/04	Stevie Wonder 5/13/50
Louis Farrakhan 5/11/33	
Alma Gluck 5/11/1884	### May 14
Martha Graham 5/11/1894	David Byrne 5/14/52
Mark Herndon 5/11/55	Bobby Darin 5/14/36
Robert Jarvik 5/11/46	Otto Klemperer 5/14/1885
Doug McClure 5/11/35	George Lucas 5/14/44
Faith Popcorn 5/11/43	Patrice Munsel 5/14/26

Shanice 5/14/73

May 15
Robert Ailes 5/15/40
Roger Ailes 5/15/40
Anna Marie Albertghetti 5/15/36
Madeleine K. Albright 5/15/37
Eddy Arnold 5/15/18
Richard Avedon 5/15/23
George Brett 5/15/53
Joseph Cotton 5/15/05
David Cronberg 5/15/43
Constance Cummings 5/15/10
Richard J. Daley 5/15/02
Dante 5/15/1265
Brian Eno 5/15/48
Jasper Johns 5/15/30
Trini Lopez 5/15/37
James Mason 5/15/09
Don Nelson 5/15/40
Katherine Ann Porter 5/15/1894
Alvin Poussaint 5/15/34
Dennis Rodman 5/15/61
Paul Rudd 5/15/40
Paul Samuelson 5/15/15
Peter Shaffer 5/15/26
Emmitt Smith 5/15/69
John Smoltz 5/15/67
Ken Venturi 5/15/31

May 16
Pierce Brosnan 5/16/53
Harry Carey, Jr. 5/16/21
Betty Carter 5/16/27
John Conyers, Jr. 5/16/29
Philippe DeMontebello 5/16/36
Henry Fonda 5/16/05
Tracey Gold 5/16/69
Woody Herman 5/16/13
Janet Jackson 5/16/66
Lainie Kazan 5/16/42
Olga Korbut 5/16/55
Liberace 5/16/19
Billy Martin 5/16/28

Jack Morris 5/16/55
Yannick Noah 5/16/60
Gabriela Sabatini 5/16/70
John Salley 5/16/64
Tori Spelling 5/16/73
Margaret Sullavan 5/16/1896
Studs Terkel 5/16/12
Thurman Thomas 5/16/66
Lowell Weicker, Jr. 5/16/31
Debra Winger 5/16/55

May 17
"Cool Papa" Bell 5/17/03
Archibald Cox 5/17/12
Jean Gabin 5/17/04
Dennis Hopper 5/17/36
George Johnson 5/17/53
Ayatollah Khomeini 5/17/00
Jon Koncak 5/17/63
Sugar Ray Leonard 5/17/56
Taj Mahal 5/17/42
Danny Manning 5/17/66
Brigit Nilsson 5/17/18
Dennis Potter 5/17/35
Bob Saget 5/17/56
Maureen O'Sullian 5/17/11
Kathleen Sullivan 5/17/53

May 18
Pierre Balmain 5/18/14
Joseph Bonsall 5/18/48
Richard Brooks 5/18/12
Frank Capra 5/18/1897
Perry Como 5/18/12
Patrick Dennis 5/18/21
Margot Fontegn 5/18/19
Margot Fonteyn 5/18/19
Dwayne Hickman 5/18/34
Reggie Jackson 5/18/46
Jacob Javits 5/18/04
Robert Morse 5/18/31
Pope John Paul II 5/18/20
Ezio Pinza 5/18/1892
Pernell Roberts 5/18/30

Brooks Robinson 5/18/37
Jean-Louis Roux 5/18/23
Warren Rudman 5/18/30
Anthony Storr 5/18/20
George Strait 5/18/52
Sam Vincent 5/18/63

May 19
Nora Ephron 5/19/41
David Hartman 5/19/35
John Hopkins 5/19/1795
Grace Jones 5/19/52
Nancy Kwan 5/19/39
Bill Laimbeer 5/19/57
James Lehrer 5/19/34
Frank Lorenzo 5/19/40
Archie Manning 5/19/49
Nellie Melba 5/19/1859
Ho Chi Minh 5/19/1890
Peter Townshend 5/19/45
Malcolm X 5/19/25

May 20
Cher 5/20/46
Joe Cocker 5/20/44
Moshe Dayan 5/20/15
Jimmy Henderson 5/20/54
George Gobel 5/20/19
Hal Newhouser 5/20/21
James Stewart 5/20/08

May 21
Raymond Burr 5/21/17
Peggy Cass 5/21/25
Janet Dailey 5/21/44
Dennis Day 5/21/17
Armand Hammer 5/21/1898
Richard Hatch 5/21/46
Horace Heidt 5/21/01
Ronald Isley 5/21/41
Robert Montgomery 5/21/04
Ara Parseghian 5/21/23
Ron Reagan 5/21/58
Harold Robbins 5/21/16

Leo Sayer 5/21/48
Mr. T 5/21/52
Fats Waller 5/21/04

May 22
Charles Aznavour 5/22/24
Richard Benjamin 5/22/38
Naomi Campbell 5/22/70
Mary Cassatt 5/22/1844
Judith Crist 5/22/22
Arthur Conan Doyle 5/22/1859
Marcus Dupree 5/22/64
Tommy John 5/22/43
Peter Nero 5/22/34
Lord Laurence Olivier 5/22/07
Barbara Parkins 5/22/42
T. Boone Pickens 5/22/28
Fredrick Ross 5/22/34
Bernard Shaw 5/22/40
Susan Strasberg 5/22/38
Richard Wagner 5/22/1813
Paul Winfield 5/22/41

May 23
Deborah Adair 5/23/52
Barbara Barrie 5/23/31
John Browning 5/23/33
Marvin Chomsky 5/23/29
Rosemary Clooney 5/23/28
Joan Collins 5/23/33
Scatman Crothers 5/23/10
Alicia DeLarrocha 5/23/23
Douglas Fairbanks 5/23/1883
Marvin Hagler 5/23/54
Anatoly Karpov 5/23/51
Helen O'Connell 5/23/21
John Payne 5/23/12
Ronald Schwary 5/23/44
Michael Serrazin 5/23/40
Artie Shaw 5/23/10

May 24
Gary Burghoff 5/24/43
Jane Byrne 5/24/34

Hector Camacho 5/24/62
Roger Caras 5/24/28
Rosanne Cash 5/24/55
Tommy Chong 5/24/38
Joe Dumars 5/24/63
Bob Dylan................................. 5/24/41
Patti Labelle 5/24/44
Jean Paul Marat 5/24/1743
Siobhan McKenna 5/24/22
Harold Melvin 5/24/41
Wilburn Mills 5/24/09
James Mora 5/24/35
S.I. Newhouse...................... 5/24/1895
Frank Oz.................................. 5/24/44
Lilli Palmer 5/24/14
Priscilla Presley 5/24/45
Coleman Young 5/24/18
Queen Victoria 5/24/1819
Mai Zefferling.......................... 5/24/25

May 25

Claude Akins........................... 5/25/18
Bela Bartok 5/25/1881
Steve Cochran........................... 5/25/17
Jessi Colter 5/25/47
Jeanne Crain 5/25/25
Hal David................................. 5/25/21
Miles Davis 5/25/26
John Gregory Dunne 5/25/32
Ralph Waldo Emerson 5/25/1803
Kendall Gill.............................. 5/25/68
Tom Glavin 5/25/66
Tom T. Hall 5/25/36
K.C. Jones 5/25/32
Jamaica Kincaid...................... 5/25/49
Michael Lally 5/25/42
Robert Ludlum 5/25/27
Ian McKellen............................ 5/25/39
Lindsey Nelson 5/25/19
Bojangles Robinson............... 5/25/1878
Connie Selleca 5/25/55
Beverly Sills 5/25/29
Marshall Tito 5/25/1892
Gene Tunney 5/25/1898

Leslie Uggams 5/25/43
Karen Valentine 5/25/47
John Weitz................................. 5/25/23

May 26

James Arness 5/26/23
Jacques Bergerac 5/26/27
Peter Cushing 5/26/13
Pamela Grier 5/26/49
Aldo Gucci 5/26/09
Al Jolson 5/26/1886
Dr. Jack Kevorkian.................... 5/26/28
Lenny Kravitz 5/26/64
Peggy Lee 5/26/20
Paul Lukas 5/26/1894
Alec McCowen 5/26/26
Tom McMillens 5/26/52
Robert Morley 5/26/08
Brent Musburger....................... 5/26/39
Stevie Nicks 5/26/48
Sally Ride 5/26/51
Jay Silverheels 5/26/22
Teresa Strates........................... 5/26/39
Norma Talmadge 5/26/1897
Philip Michael Thomas 5/26/49
John Wayne............................... 5/26/07
Hank Williams, Jr. 5/26/49

May 27

John Barth 5/27/30
Todd Bridges 5/27/65
Allen Carr 5/27/41
Pat Cash................................... 5/27/65
John Cheever 5/27/12
Christopher Dodd 5/27/44
Isadora Duncan 5/27/1878
Louis Gossett, Jr. 5/27/36
Dashiell Hammett................. 5/27/1894
Wild Bill Hickok................... 5/27/1837
Tony Hillerman 5/27/25
Hubert Humphrey 5/27/11
Lindy Infante 5/27/40
Henry Kissinger 5/27/23
Teddy Kolleck 5/27/11

Christopher Lee 5/27/22
Ramsey Lewis 5/27/35
Lee Ann Meriwether 5/27/35
Vincent Price 5/27/11
Sumner Redstone 5/27/23
William Sessions 5/27/30
Sam Snead 5/27/12
Frank Thomas 5/27/68
Bruce Weitz 5/27/43
Herman Wouk 5/27/15

May 28

Carroll Baker 5/28/35
Stephen Birmingham 5/28/31
Dietrich Fischer-Dieskau 5/28/25
Ian Fleming 5/28/08
Kirk Gibson 5/28/57
Beth Howland 5/28/47
John Karlen 5/28/33
Gladys Knight 5/28/44
Sandra Locke 5/28/47
Walker Percy 5/28/16
Dionne Quintuplets 5/28/34
Glen Rice 5/28/67
David Shula 5/28/59
Jim Thorpe 5/28/1888
Martha Vickers 5/28/25
Jerry West 5/28/38
Irwin Winkler 5/28/31

May 29

Iris Adrian 5/29/13
Annette Bening 5/29/58
Helmut Berger 5/29/44
Kevin Conway 5/29/42
Paul Ehrlich 5/29/32
Anthony Geary 5/29/49
Patrick Henry 5/29/1736
John Hinckley, Jr. 5/29/55
Bob Hope 5/29/03
LaToya Jackson 5/29/56
John F. Kennedy 5/29/17
Beatrice Lillie 5/29/1898
Burt Richards 5/29/30

Felix Rohatyn 5/29/28
Herb Shriner 5/29/18
Al Unser 5/29/39
Faye Vincent 5/29/38
Josef Von Sternberg 5/29/1894
Lisa Whelchel 5/29/63
Iannis Xenakis 5/29/22

May 30

Mel Blanc 5/30/08
Keir Dullea 5/30/36
Stepin Fetchit 5/30/02
Benny Goodman 5/30/09
Howard Hawks 5/30/1898
Christine Jorgensen 5/30/26
Wynonna Judd 5/30/64
Meredith MacRae 5/30/44
Ted McGinley 5/30/58
Michael J. Pollard 5/30/39
Gale Sayers 5/30/43
Cornelia Otis Skinner 5/30/01
Irving Thalberg 5/30/1899
Clint Walker 5/30/27

May 31

Fred Allen 5/31/1894
Don Ameche 5/31/08
Edgar Paul Barselou 5/31/22
Tom Berenger 5/31/50
Clint Eastwood 5/31/30
Denholm Elliott 5/31/22
Sharon Gless 5/31/43
Cliff Gorman 5/31/63
Gregory Harrison 5/31/50
Jim Hutton 5/31/38
Joe Namath 5/31/43
Johnny Paycheck 5/31/41
Norman Vincent Peale 5/31/1898
Prince Rainer 5/31/23
Brooke Shields 5/31/65
Shirley Verrett 5/31/33
Walt Whitman 5/31/1819
Edward Bennett Williams 5/31/20
Peter Yarrow 5/31/38

June 1

Rene Auberjonois	6/1/40
David Berkowitz	6/1/53
Pat Boone	6/1/34
Clive Brook	6/1/1887
Joan Caulfield	6/1/22
Morgan Freeman	6/1/37
Andy Griffith	6/1/26
Lisa Hartman	6/1/56
John B. Hood	6/1/1831
Reverend Ike	6/1/35
Cleavon Little	6/1/39
Peter Masterson	6/1/34
Marilyn Monroe	6/1/26
Frank Morgan	6/1/1890
Jonathan Pryce	6/1/47
John Randolph, Jr.	6/1/15
Nelson Riddle	6/1/21
Tom Sneva	6/1/48
John Van Druten	6/1/04
Frederica Von Stade	6/1/45
Sir Frank Whittle	6/1/07
Alan Wilder	6/1/63
Ron Wood	6/1/47
Edward Woodward	6/1/30
Brigham Young	6/1/1801

June 2

Rick Astley	6/2/66
Charles Conrad, Jr.	6/2/30
Sir Edward Elgar	6/2/1857
Charles Haid	6/2/43
Marvin Hamlisch	6/2/44
Thomas Hardy	6/2/1840
Lenora Mae Hill	6/2/37
Hedda Hopper	6/2/1890
Stacy Keach	6/2/41
Sally Kellerman	6/2/37
Arthur MacArthur	6/2/1845
Jerry Mathers	6/2/48
Milo O'Shea	6/2/26
Clarence Page	6/2/47
Craig Stadler	6/2/53

Mike Todd	6/2/07
Charlie Watts	6/2/41
Johnny Weissmuller	6/2/04
Garo Yepremian	6/2/44

June 3

Josephine Baker	6/3/06
Raul Castro	6/3/31
Ellen Corby	6/3/13
Billy Cunningham	6/3/43
Tony Curtis	6/3/25
Jefferson Davis	6/3/1808
Colleen Dewhurst	6/3/26
Maurice Evans	6/3/01
Allen Ginsberg	6/3/26
Paulette Goddard	6/3/11
Leo Gorcey	6/3/15
Hale Irwin	6/3/45
Bert Lance	6/3/31
Curtis Mayfield	6/3/42
Larry McMurtry	6/3/36
Ransom Eli Olds	6/3/1864
Jan Peerce	6/3/04

June 4

Luther Adler	6/4/03
Gene Barry	6/4/22
Clara Blandick	6/4/1880
Charles Collingwood	6/4/17
David Keith	6/4/56
Bruce Dern	6/4/36
William Elliott	6/4/34
Freddie Fender	6/4/37
Samuel L. Gravely, Jr.	6/4/22
Andrea Jaeger	6/4/65
Judith Malina	6/4/26
Xavier McDaniel	6/4/63
Robert Merrill	6/4/19
Howard Metzenbaum	6/4/17
Tony Pena	6/4/57
Parker Stevenson	6/4/52
Dennis Weaver	6/4/25
Dr. Ruth Westheimer	6/4/28

June 5
Chad Allen 6/5/74
Bill Boyd 6/5/1898
Thomas Chippendale 6/5/1718
Jacques Demy 6/5/31
Ken Follett 6/5/49
Kenny G 6/5/56
Madam Chiang Kai-Shek 6/5/1857
John Maynard Keynes 6/5/1883
Robert Lansing 6/5/29
Federico Garcia Lorca 6/5/1899
Bill Moyers 6/5/34
Bob Probert 6/5/65
Tony Richardson 6/5/29
Rosalind Russell 6/5/12
Cornelius Ryan 6/5/20
Adams Smith 6/5/1723
Mark Wahlberg 6/5/71

June 6
Walter Abel 6/6/1898
Sandra Bernhard 6/6/55
Gary U.S. Bonds 6/6/39
David Bonior 6/6/45
Bjorn Borg 6/6/56
Mark Calcavecchin 6/6/60
Gilbert Cates 6/6/34
George Deukmejian 6/6/28
Bill Dickey 6/6/07
David Dukes 6/6/45
Robert Englund 6/6/49
Harvey Fierstein 6/6/54
Ted Flicker 6/6/30
Roy Innis 6/6/34
Kirk Kerkorian 6/6/17
Jimmy Lunceford 6/6/02
Thomas Mann 6/6/1875
Lorrie Morgan 6/6/59
Amanda Pays 6/6/59
Alexander Pushkin 6/6/1799
T.K. (Tom) Ryan 6/6/26
David R. Scott 6/6/32
Diego Velazquez 6/6/1599
Billie Whitelaw 6/6/32

June 7
Gwendolyn Brooks 6/7/17
Paul Gauguin 6/7/1848
Nikki Giovanni 6/7/43
Rocky Graziano 6/7/22
Tom Jones (singer) 6/7/40
David Lundstrom 6/7/47
Dean Martin 6/7/17
Thurman Munson 6/7/47
Liam Neeson 6/7/52
Prince 6/7/58
Cazzie Russell 6/7/44
George Szell 6/7/1897
Jessica Tandy 6/7/09
Debora Tannen 6/7/45

June 8
Herb Adderley 6/8/39
Emanuel Ax 6/8/49
Barbara Bush 6/8/25
Francis Crick 6/8/16
James Darren 6/8/36
Willie Davenport 6/8/43
George Kirby 6/8/23
Leroy Neiman 6/8/26
Lyn Nofziger 6/8/24
Sara Paretsky 6/8/47
Robert Preston 6/8/18
Charles Reade 6/8/1814
Butch Reynolds 6/8/64
Nick Rhodes 6/8/62
Joan Rivers 6/8/33
William Rukeyser 6/8/39
Boz Scagg 6/8/44
Robert Schumann 6/8/1810
Nancy Sinatra, Jr. 6/8/40
Alexis Smith 6/8/21
Jerry Stiller 6/8/26
Bonnie Tyler 6/8/53
Keenan Ivory Wayans 6/8/58
Byron White 6/8/17
Frank Lloyd Wright 6/8/1867
Dana Wynter 6/8/32

June 9

George Axelrod	6/9/22
Robert Cummings	6/9/10
Johnny Depp	6/9/63
Michael J. Fox	6/9/61
Mona Freeman	6/9/26
Marvin Kalb	6/9/30
Jackie Mason	6/9/30
Robert McNamara	6/9/16
Carl August Nielsen	6/9/1865
Dave Parker	6/9/51
Les Paul	6/9/16
John Howard Payne	6/9/1791
Peter the Great	6/9/1672
Cole Porter	6/9/1892
Wayman Tisdair	6/9/64
Fred Waring	6/9/00
Jackie Wilson	6/9/32

June 10

F. Lee Bailey	6/10/33
Saul Bellow	6/10/15
Philip Caputo	6/10/41
Gustava Courbet	6/10/1819
Dan Fouts	6/10/51
Judy Garland	6/10/22
Jeff Greenfield	6/10/43
June Haver	6/10/26
Sessue Hayakawa	6/10/1889
Howlin Wolf	6/10/10
Frederick Lowe	6/10/04
Hattie McDaniel	6/10/1895
Jim McDivitt	6/10/29
Barry Morse	6/10/18
Prince Philip	6/10/21
Terence Rattigan	6/10/11
Maurice Sendak	6/10/28
Andrew Stevens	6/10/55

June 11

Adrienne Barbeau	6/11/45
Michael Cacoyannis	6/11/22
Julia M. Cameron	6/11/1815
Henry Cisneros	6/11/47
Jacques Cousteau	6/11/10
Chad Everett	6/11/37
Athol Fugard	6/11/32
Robert Hutton	6/11/20
Frank King	6/11/1883
Vince Lombardi	6/11/13
Paul Mellon	6/11/07
Joe Montana	6/11/56
Charles Rangel	6/11/38
Hazel Scott	6/11/20
Rise Stevens	6/11/13
Jackie Stewart	6/11/39
Richard Strauss	6/11/1864
William Styron	6/11/25
Richard Todd	6/11/19
Gene Wilder	6/11/34

June 12

Marv Albert	6/12/43
Samuel Z. Arkoff	6/12/18
Nicole Berger	6/12/35
Timothy Busfield	6/12/57
George Bush	6/12/24
Chick Corea	6/12/41
Vic Damone	6/12/28
Anthony Eden	6/12/1897
Anne Frank	6/12/29
Uta Hagen	6/12/19
Russell Hayden	6/12/12
Rona Jaffe	6/12/32
Oliver Knussen	6/12/52
William Lundigan	6/12/14
Jim Nabors	6/12/32
David Rockefeller	6/12/15
John A. Roebling	6/12/1806

June 13

Tim Allen	6/13/53
Luis Alvarez	6/13/11
Don Budge	6/13/15
Bettina Bunge	6/13/63
Christo	6/13/35

Ralph Edwards 6/13/13
Red Granger 6/13/03
Ben Johnson 6/13/18
Paul Lynde 6/13/26
Malcolm McDowell 6/13/43
Chuck Nevitt 6/13/59
Eleanor Holmes Norton 6/13/38
Basil Rathbone 6/13/1892
Ally Sheedy 6/13/62
Joseph Stella 6/13/1880
Richard Thomas 6/13/51
Mark Van Doren 6/13/1894
William Butler Yates 6/13/1865

June 14

May Allison 6/14/1895
Gene Barry 6/14/22
Margaret Bourke-White 6/14/04
Major Bowes 6/14/1874
Cy Coleman 6/14/29
Vince Evans 6/14/55
Marla Gibbs 6/14/31
Steffi Graf 6/14/69
Eric Heiden 6/14/58
Burl Ives 6/14/09
Jerzy Kosinski 6/14/33
Christopher Lehmann-Haupt . 6/14/34
Dorothy McGuire 6/14/18
Eddie Mekka 6/14/52
Don Newcombe 6/14/26
Sam Perkins 6/14/61
Pierre Salinger 6/14/25
Mona Simpson 6/14/57
Harriet Beecher Stowe 6/14/1811
Donald Trump 6/14/46
Sam Wanamaker 6/14/19

June 15

Yuri Andropov 6/15/14
Dusty Baker 6/15/49
Jim Belush 6/15/54
Wade Boggs 6/15/58
Tony Coelho 6/15/42
Courteney Cox 6/15/64

Mario Cuomo 6/15/32
Erik Erikson 6/15/02
Erroll Garner 6/15/21
Terri Gibbs 6/15/54
Helen Hunt 6/15/63
Waylon Jennings 6/15/37
Harry Langdon 6/15/1884
Harry Nilsson 6/15/41
Saul Steinberg 6/15/14
Morris Udall 6/15/22
Jim Varney 6/15/49
Billy Williams 6/15/38

June 16

Rick Adelman 6/16/46
Jack Albertson 6/16/10
Ian Buchanan 6/16/55
Roberto Duran 6/16/51
Katharine Graham 6/16/17
John Howard Griffin 6/16/20
Wally Joyner 6/16/62
Stan Laurel 6/16/1890
Eddie LeVert 6/16/42
Ilona Massey 6/16/10
Joyce Carol Oates 6/16/38
Irving Penn 6/16/17
Tree Rollins 6/16/55
Erich Segal 6/16/37
Tupac Shakur 6/16/71
Joan Van Ark 6/16/46

June 17

Ralph Bellamy 6/17/04
Red Foley 6/17/10
Newt Gingrich 6/17/43
Charles Gounod 6/17/1818
Heinz Guderian 6/17/1888
John Hersey 6/17/14
Dan Jansen 6/17/65
Barry Manilow 6/17/46
Robert Maynard 6/17/37
Joe Piscopo 6/17/51
Igor Stravinsky 6/17/1882
John Wesley 6/17/03

June 18

Sandy Alomar, Jr. 6/18/66
Eva Bartok 6/18/26
Richard Boone 6/18/17
Lou Brock 6/18/39
Sammy Cahn 6/18/13
Bud Collyer 6/18/08
Roger Ebert 6/18/42
Carol Kane 6/18/52
Keye Luke 6/18/04
Jeanette MacDonald 6/18/06
E.G. Marshall 6/18/10
Paul McCartney 6/18/42
Sylvia Porter 6/18/13
John D. Rockefeller IV 6/18/37
Isabella Rossellini 6/18/52
Bruce Smith 6/18/63
Blanche Sweet 6/18/1895
Tom Wicker 6/18/26

June 19

Pier Angeli 6/19/32
Charles Coburn 6/19/1865
Alan Cranston 6/19/14
Osamu Dazai 6/19/09
Martin Gabel 6/19/12
Lou Gehrig 6/19/03
Howard Heflin 6/19/21
Laura Z. Hobson 6/19/00
Moe Howard 6/19/1897
Vernon Jarrett 6/19/21
Louis Jourdan 6/19/20
Pauline Kael 6/19/19
Guy Lombardo 6/19/02
Nancy Marchand 6/19/28
Malcolm McDowell 6/19/43
Mildred Natwick 6/19/08
Marisa Pavan 6/19/32
Phylica Rashad 6/19/48
Gena Rowlands 6/19/36
Wallis Simpson 6/19/1896
Doug Stone 6/19/56
Kathleen Turner 6/19/54
Quincy Watts 6/19/70

Dame May Whitty 6/19/1865
Tobias Wolff 6/19/45

June 20

Danny Aiello 6/20/36
Chet Atkins 6/20/24
Edgan Bronfman 6/20/29
Charles Chesnutt 6/20/1858
Olympia Dukakis 6/20/31
Errol Flynn 6/20/09
Stephen Frears 6/20/41
John Goodman 6/20/52
Doris Hart 6/20/25
Lillian Hellman 6/20/05
Martin Landau 6/20/34
Cyndi Lauper 6/20/53
John Mahoney 6/20/40
Audie Murphy 6/20/24
Anne Murray 6/20/45
Jacques Offenbach 6/20/1819
Gail Patrick 6/20/11
Ellis Rabb 6/20/30
Lionel Richie 6/20/49
Tex Schramm 6/20/20
Helen Traubel 6/20/1899
Bob Vila 6/20/46
Andre Watts 6/20/46
Brian Wilson 6/20/42
Terence Young 6/20/15

June 21

Bruce Babbitt 6/21/38
Meredith Baxter 6/21/47
Tom Chambers 6/21/59
Derrick Coleman 6/21/67
Ray Davies 6/21/44
Michael Gross 6/21/47
Mariette Hartley 6/21/40
Al Hirschfeld 6/21/03
Judy Holliday 6/21/22
Rockwell Kent 6/21/1882
Nicole Kidman 6/21/67
Bernard Kopell 6/21/33
Juliette Lewis 6/21/73

Al Martinez 6/21/29
Kathy Mattea 6/21/59
Ken Maynard 6/21/1895
Mary McCarthy 6/21/12
Willie Mosconi 6/21/13
Reinhold Niebuhr 6/21/1892
Robert Pastorelli 6/21/54
Jane Russell 6/21/21
Francoise Sagan 6/21/35
Jean-Paul Sartre 6/21/05
Maureen Stapleton 6/21/25
Dorothy Stickney 6/21/00
Rick Sutcliffe 6/21/56
Peter Weir 6/21/44
Prince William 6/21/82

June 22

Buddy Adler 6/22/09
Bill Blass 6/22/22
Ed Bradley 6/22/41
Klaus Marie Brandauer 6/22/44
Clyde Drexler 6/22/62
Dianne Feinstein 6/22/33
Rose Kennedy 6/22/1890
Kris Kristofferson 6/22/37
Anne Morrow Lindbergh 6/22/06
Pete Maravich 6/22/48
Joseph Papp 6/22/21
Tracy Pollan 6/22/62
Freddie Prinze 6/22/54
Erich Marie Remarque 6/22/1898
Todd Rundgren 6/22/40
Dr. William Scholl 6/22/1882
Meryl Streep 6/22/49
Mike Todd 6/22/07
Lindsay Wagner 6/22/49
Ralph Waite 6/22/29
Billy Wilder 6/22/06

June 23

Anna Akhmatova 6/23/1889
Jean Anouilh 6/23/10
Richard D. Bach 6/23/36
June Carter-Cash 6/23/29

Prince Edward 6/23/1894
Bob Fosse 6/23/27
Nicholas Gage 6/23/39
Alfred Kinsey 6/23/1894
Ted Lapidus 6/23/29
James Levine 6/23/43
Edouard Michelin 6/23/1859
Art Modell 6/23/25
Dennis Price 6/23/15
Wilma Rudolph 6/23/40
Ted Shackelford 6/23/46
Clarence Thomas 6/23/48
Irene Worth 6/23/16

June 24

Jeff Beck 6/24/44
Arthur Brown 6/24/44
Billy Casper 6/24/31
Claude Chabrol 6/24/30
Norman Cousins 6/24/15
Jack Dempsey 6/24/1895
E.I. DuPont 6/24/1771
Mick Fleetwood 6/24/47
Chief Dan George 6/24/1899
Phil Harris 6/24/06
Sam Jones 6/24/33
Josephine (Bonaparte) 6/24/1763
Michele Lee 6/24/42
George Pataki 6/24/45
Ralph Reed 6/24/61
Robert Reich 6/24/46
Peter Weller 6/24/47

June 25

George Abbott 6/25/1887
Jack Carter 6/25/23
Phyllis George 6/25/49
Peter Lind Hayes 6/25/15
Roger Livesey 6/25/06
June Lockhart 6/25/25
Sidney Lumet 6/25/24
James Meredith 6/25/33
George Michael 6/25/63
Dikembe Mutombo 6/25/66

George Orwell 6/25/03
Willis Reed 6/25/42
Carly Simon 6/25/45
Jimmie Walker 6/25/48

June 26
Peal Buck 6/26/1892
Billy Davis, Jr. 6/26/40
Abner Doubleday 6/26/1819
Jean Eagels 6/26/1894
Jerome Kersey 6/26/62
Bill Lear 6/26/02
Greg Lemond 6/26/61
Peter Lorre 6/26/04
Clarence Lovejoy 6/26/1894
Chris O'Donnell 6/26/70
Eleanor Parker 6/26/22
Charles Robb 6/26/39
Jerry Schatzberg 6/26/27
Robert Seigel 6/26/47
Babe Didrickson Zaharias 6/26/12

June 27
Isabella Adjani 6/27/55
Bruce Babbitt 6/27/38
Roger Stuart Berlind 6/27/30
Paul F. Conrad 6/27/24
Gary Crosby 6/27/33
Julia Duffy 6/27/51
Paul Laurence Dunbar 6/27/1872
Craig Hodges 6/27/60
Bruce Johnson 6/27/44
Norma Kamali 6/27/45
Bob Keeshan 6/27/27
Helen Keller 6/27/1880
Krzysztof Kieslowski 6/27/41
Catherine Lacoste 6/27/45
Alice McDermott 6/27/53
John McIntire 6/27/07
Anna Moffo 6/27/34
H. Ross Perot 6/27/30
Rico Petrocelli 6/27/43
Lionel Richie 6/27/49
Robby Rosa 6/27/69

June 28
Eric Ambler 6/28/09
Kathy Bates 6/28/48
Don Baylor 6/28/49
Danielle Brisebois 6/28/69
Mel Brooks 6/28/28
John Cusack 6/28/66
John Dillinger 6/28/02
John Elway 6/28/60
Mark Grace 6/28/64
Henry VIII 6/28/1491
A.E. Hotchner 6/28/20
Bobby Hurley 6/28/71
Jeff Malone 6/28/61
Ashley Montagu 6/28/05
Pat Morita 6/28/33
Leon Panetta 6/28/38
Gilda Radner 6/28/46
Jean Jacques Rousseau 6/28/1712
Peter Paul Rubens 6/28/1577
Otis Skinner 6/28/1858

June 29
Gary Busey 6/29/44
Stokely Carmichael 6/29/41
Joan Davis 6/29/08
Antonine de Saint Exupery 6/29/00
Dan Dierdorf 6/29/49
Amanda Donohoe 6/29/62
Nelson Eddy 6/29/01
Oriana Fallaci 6/29/30
Jeff Freilich 6/29/48
Fred Grandy 6/29/48
Pedro Guerrero 6/29/56
Nancy Kassebaum 6/29/32
Hermon Killebrow 6/29/36
Carl Levin 6/29/34
Richard Lewis 6/29/47
Frank Loesser 6/29/10
Czeslaw Milosz 6/29/11
Claude Montana 6/29/49
Slim Pickens 6/29/19
Hiram Powers 6/29/1805
John Toland 6/29/12

Ruth Warrick 6/29/16

June 30
Madge Bellamy 6/30/00
Harry Blackstone 6/30/34
Nancy Dussault 6/30/36
David Alan Grier 6/30/56
Susan Hayward 6/30/19
Lena Horne 6/30/17
Mary Loughlin 6/30/56
Geoffrey Moss 6/30/38
Buddy Rich 6/30/17
Thomas Sowell 6/30/30
Mike Tyson 6/30/66
David Wayne 6/30/14

July 1
Wally "Famous" Amos 7/1/36
Daryl Anderson 7/1/51
Dan Aykroyd 7/1/52
Karen Black 7/1/42
Genevieve Bujold 7/1/42
James M. Cain 7/1/1892
Leslie Caron 7/1/31
Andre Crouch 7/1/42
Olivia DeHavilland 7/1/16
Princess Diana 7/1/61
Piero Mimitri 7/1/33
Jamie Farr 7/1/34
Farley Granger 7/1/25
Deborah Harry 7/1/45
Charles Hatcher 7/1/39
Estee Lauder 7/1/08
Charles Laughton 7/1/1899
Carl Lewis 7/1/61
Jean Marsh 7/1/34
Sidney Pollack 7/1/34
Sally Quinn 7/1/41
Jean-Pierre Rampal 7/1/22
Guy Raymond 7/1/11
Twyla Tharp 7/1/41
William Wyler 7/1/02

July 2
Jose Canseco 7/2/64
Medgar Evers 7/2/25
Barry Gray 7/2/16
Tyrone Guthrie 7/2/00
Jerry Hall 7/2/56
Hermann Hesse 7/2/1877
Polly Holliday 7/2/37
Ahmad Jamal 7/2/30
Luci Baines Johnson 7/2/47
Franz Kafka 7/2/1883
Rene Lacoste 7/2/05
Thurgood Marshall 7/2/08
James McNichol 7/2/61
Brock Peters 7/2/27
Richard Petty 7/2/37
Dan Rowan 7/2/22
Ron Silver 7/2/46
John Sununu 7/2/39
R. David Thomas 7/2/32

July 3
Moises Alou 7/3/66
Laura Branigan 7/3/57
Betty Buckley 7/3/47
George M. Cohan 7/3/1878
Tom Cruise 7/3/62
Brigitte Fassbaender 7/3/39
Pete Fountain 7/3/30
Dorothy Kilgallen 7/3/13
Stavros Niarchos 7/3/09
Neil O'Donnell 7/3/66
Geraldo Rivera 7/3/43
Ken Russell 7/3/27
George Sanders 7/3/06
David Shire 7/3/37
Tom Stoppard 7/3/37
Aaron Tippin 7/3/58
Montel Williams 7/3/56

July 4
Louis Armstrong 7/4/00
Stephen Boyd 7/4/28

Calvin Coolidge 7/4/1872
Al Davis 7/4/29
Rube Goldberg 7/4/1883
Virginia Graham 7/4/12
Harvey Grant 7/4/65
Horace Grant 7/4/65
Nathaniel Hawthorne 7/4/1804
Ann Landers 7/4/18
Meyer Lansky 7/4/02
Henri LeConte 7/4/63
Gina Lollobrigida 7/4/28
Louis B. Mayer 7/4/1885
Mitch Miller 7/4/11
Tokyo Rose 7/4/16
Eva Marie Saint 7/4/24
Pam Shriver 7/4/62
Neil Simon 7/4/27
George Steinbrenner 7/4/30
Abigail Van Buren 7/4/18
Hiram Walker 7/4/1816
Bill Withers 7/4/38

July 5
P.T. Barnum 7/5/1810
Jean Cocteau 7/5/1889
Eliot Feld 7/5/42
Rich "Goose" Gossage 7/5/51
Katherine Helmond 7/5/34
Shirley Knight 7/5/36
Huey Lewis 7/5/51
Henry Cabot Lodge 7/5/02
James Lofton 7/5/56
John McKay 7/5/23
Victor Navasky 7/5/32
Julie Nixon-Eisenhower 7/5/48
Beatrix Potter 7/5/1866
Cecil Rhodes 7/5/1853
Milburn Stone 7/5/04

July 6
Vladimir Ashkenazy 7/6/37
Ned Beatty 7/6/37
Louie Bellson 7/6/24
Valerie Brisco-Hooks 7/6/60

Sebastian Cabot 7/6/18
The Dalai Lama 7/6/35
Fred Dryer 7/6/46
Grant Goodeve 7/6/52
Merv Griffin 7/6/25
Shelley Hack 7/6/49
Bill Haley 7/6/25
Janet Leigh 7/6/27
Pat Paulsen 7/6/27
Nancy Reagan 7/6/21
Della Reese 7/6/32
William Schallert 7/6/22
Sylvester Stallone 7/6/46
Burt Ward 7/6/45
Jamie Wyeth 7/6/46

July 7
Pierre Cardin 7/7/22
Marc Chagall 7/7/1887
Ezzard Charles 7/7/21
George Cukor 7/7/1899
Vittorio DeSica 7/7/02
Shelly Duvall 7/7/49
Vincent Edwards 7/7/28
William Kunstler 7/7/19
Gian Carlo Menotti 7/7/11
Lawrence O'Brien 7/7/17
Satchel Paige 7/7/06
Ralph Sampson 7/7/60
Doc Severinsen 7/7/27
Ringo Starr 7/7/40

July 8
Roone Arledge 7/8/31
Kevin Bacon 7/8/58
Kim Darby 7/8/48
John Dingell 7/8/26
Billy Eckstine 7/8/14
Faye Emerson 7/8/17
Anjelica Huston 7/8/51
Louis Jordan 7/8/08
Steve Lawrence 7/8/35
Barbara Loden 7/8/37
Anna Quindlen 7/8/53

Raffi 7/8/48
John D. Rockefeller 7/8/1839
Nelson Rockefeller 7/8/08
George Romney 7/8/07
Craig Stevens 7/8/18
Jerry Vale 7/8/32
Marianne Williamson 7/8/52

July 9
Ed Ames 7/9/27
Barbara Cartland 7/9/01
Brian Denneny 7/9/40
Tom Hanks 7/9/56
David Hockney 7/9/37
Kelly McGillis 7/9/57
Wally Post 7/9/29
O.J. Simpson 7/9/47
Jimmy Smits 7/9/58
John Tesh 7/9/52

July 10
Nick Adams 7/10/31
Arthur Ashe 7/10/43
Nell Walden Blaine 7/10/22
David Brinkley 7/10/20
Mary Bunting 7/10/10
Carleton Carpenter 7/10/26
Roger Craig 7/10/60
Andre Dawson 7/10/54
Giorgio deChirico 7/10/1880
David Dinkins 7/10/27
Jeff Donnell 7/10/21
John Gilbert 7/10/1897
Arlo Guthrie 7/10/47
Fred Gwynne 7/10/26
Richard Hatcher 7/10/33
H.J. Heinz III 7/10/08
Jerry Herman 7/10/33
Jean Kerr 7/10/23
Jake LaMotta 7/10/21
Sue Lyon 7/10/46
Hal McRae 7/10/45
Thomas Mitchell 7/10/1892
Marcel Proust 7/10/1871

Mark Shera 7/10/49
Eunice Kennedy Shriver 7/10/20
Virginia Wade 7/10/45

July 11
John Quincy Adams 7/11/1767
Giorgio Armani 7/11/34
Sally Blane 7/11/10
Mattiwilda Dobbs 7/11/25
Gene Evans 7/11/22
Nicolai Gedda 7/11/25
Tab Hunter 7/11/31
Bonnie Pointer 7/11/51
Richie Sambora 7/11/59
Brett Somers 7/11/27
Leon Spinks 7/11/53
Rod Strickland 7/11/66
Beverly Todd 7/11/55
Suzanne Vega 7/11/59
Walter Wanger 7/11/1894
Sela Ward 7/11/56
E.B. White 7/11/1899

July 12
Keith Andes 7/12/20
Milton Berle 7/12/08
Tod Browning 7/12/1884
Yul Brynner 7/12/20
Julius Caesar .... 7/12/100 BC
Van Cliburn 7/12/34
Bill Cosby 7/12/37
Dolly Dollar 7/12/62
Kirsten Flagstad 7/12/1895
Harrison Ford 7/12/42
Buckminster Fuller 7/12/1895
Oscar Hammerstein 7/12/1895
Mark Hatfield 7/12/22
Jean Hersholt 7/12/1886
Cheryl Ladd 7/12/51
Christie McVie 7/12/43
Amadeo Modigliani 7/12/1884
Pablo Neruda 7/12/04
Vera Ralston 7/12/19
Richard Simmons 7/12/48

Jay Thomas 7/12/48
Henry David Thoreau 7/12/1817
Donald Westlake 7/12/33
Andrew Wyeth 7/12/17
Kristi Yamaguchi 7/12/71

July 13
Carlo Bergonzi 7/13/24
Sidney Blackmer 7/13/1896
Cheech (Richard Martin) 7/13/46
Bob Crane 7/13/28
Cameron Crowe 7/13/57
Bosley Crowther 7/13/05
Father Flanagan 7/13/1886
Dave Garroway 7/13/13
Jack Kemp 7/13/35
Paul Prudhomme 7/13/40
Erno Rubik 7/13/44
Michael Spinks 7/13/56
Patrick Stewart 7/13/40
Spud Webb 7/13/63
James Wooten 7/13/37

July 14
Annabella 7/14/12
Boy George 7/14/61
Polly Bergen 7/14/30
Ingmar Bergman 7/14/18
John Chancellor 7/14/27
"Happy" Chandler 7/14/1898
Douglas Edwards 7/14/17
Lee Elder 7/14/34
Gerald Ford 7/14/13
David Gordon 7/14/36
Roosevelt Grier 7/14/32
Woody Guthrie 7/14/12
Bill Hanna 7/14/10
Arthur Laurents 7/14/18
Dale Robertson 7/14/23
Jerry Rubin 7/14/38
Stan Shaw 7/14/52
Isaac Bushevis Singer 7/14/04
Harry Dean Stanton 7/14/26
Irving Stone 7/14/03

Steve Stone 7/14/47
Terry Thomas 7/14/11
Robin Ventura 7/14/67

July 15
Kim Alexis 7/15/60
Jean-Bertrand Aristide 7/15/53
Richard Armour 7/15/06
Julian Bream 7/15/33
Joycelyn Bell Burnell 7/15/43
Brian Austin Green 7/15/73
Alex Karras 7/15/35
Ken Kercheval 7/15/35
Iris Murdoch 7/15/19
Virginia Peters 7/15/24
Linda Ronstadt 7/15/46
John Stallworth 7/15/52
Jan-Michael Vincent 7/15/44
Patrick Wayne 7/15/39
Forest Whitaker 7/15/61

July 16
Ruben Blades 7/16/48
Phoebe Cates 7/16/63
Margaret Smith Court 7/16/42
Mary Baker Eddy 7/16/1821
Barnard Hughes 7/16/15
Shoeless Joe Jackson 7/16/1887
Charles Joffe 7/16/29
Jimmy Johnson 7/16/43
Trygve Lie 7/16/1896
Bess Myerson 7/16/24
Terry Pendleton 7/16/60
Owen Rachleff 7/16/34
Ginger Rogers 7/16/11
Barry Sanders 7/16/68
Charles Smith 7/16/65
Barbara Stanwyck 7/16/07
Richard Thornburgh 7/16/32
Pinchas Zukerman 7/16/48

July 17
Hardy Amies 7/17/09
Lucie Arnaz 7/17/51

Lou Boudreau	7/17/17
James Cagney	7/17/1899
Diahann Carroll	7/17/35
John Carroll	7/17/05
Calbert Cheaney	7/17/71
Cass Daley	7/17/15
Marcell Dalio	7/17/00
Phyllis Diller	7/17/17
Erie Stanley Gardner	7/17/1889
William Gargan	7/17/05
Gale Garnett	7/17/42
Nancy Giles	7/17/60
David Hasselhoff	7/17/52
Connie Hawkins	7/17/42
Daryle Lamonica	7/17/41
Nicolette Larson	7/17/52
Art Linkletter	7/17/12
Brigitte Nielsen	7/17/63
Camilla Parker-Bowles	7/17/47
Phoebe Snow	7/17/52
Eleanor Steber	7/17/16
Donald Sutherland	7/17/34
Bryan Trottier	7/17/56
Bruce Wade	7/17/51
Jessamyn West	7/17/02

July 18

Richard Branson	7/18/50
James Brolin	7/18/41
Dick Button	7/18/29
Dennis Cole	7/18/43
Hume Cronyn	7/18/11
Richard Dix	7/18/1894
Nick Faldo	7/18/57
John Glenn	7/18/21
Anfernee Hardaway	7/18/72
S.I. Hayakawa	7/18/06
Gene Lockhart	7/18/1891
Nelson Mandela	7/18/18
Kurt Masur	7/18/27
Elizabeth McGovern	7/18/61
Harriet Nelson	7/18/12
Clifford Odet	7/18/06
Calvin Peete	7/18/43

Martha Reeves	7/18/41
Ricky Skagg	7/18/54
Red Skelton	7/18/13
Hunter Thompson	7/18/39
Lupe Velez	7/18/07
Chill Wills	7/18/03
Yevgeny Yevtushenko	7/18/33

July 19

Philip Agee	7/19/35
Lizzie Borden	7/19/1860
Vikki Carr	7/19/41
Lilly Damita	7/19/01
Edgar Degas	7/19/1834
Atom Egoyan	7/19/60
Helen Gallagher	7/19/26
Ron Glass	7/19/45
Pat Hingle	7/19/24
George McGovern	7/19/22
Ilie Nastase	7/19/49
E.P. Snow	7/19/05
Duchess of Windsor	7/19/1896

July 20

Lola Albright	7/20/24
Theda Bara	7/20/1890
Kim Carnes	7/20/46
Michael Collins	7/20/69
Chuck Daly	7/20/33
Elizabeth Dole	7/20/36
Sally Ann Howes	7/20/30
John Kleiser	7/20/46
Diana Rigg	7/20/38
Carlos Santana	7/20/47
T.G. Sheppard	7/20/44
Natalie Wood	7/20/39

July 21

Les Aspin	7/21/38
Paul Burke	7/21/26
Hart Crane	7/21/1899
Henry Ellard	7/21/61
John Gardner	7/21/33
Ernest Hemingway	7/21/1899

Edward Herrmann 7/21/43
Norman Jewison 7/21/26
Allyn Joslyn 7/21/01
Frances Keyes 7/21/1885
Don Knotts 7/21/24
Gene Littler 7/21/30
Jon Lovitz 7/21/57
Marshall McLuhan 7/21/11
Jonathan Miller......................... 7/21/34
Janet Reno 7/21/38
C. Aubrey Smith 7/21/1863
Kay Starr 7/21/22
Isaac Stern 7/21/20
Cat Stevens 7/21/48
Paul Wellstone 7/21/44
Robin Williams......................... 7/21/52

July 22

Licia Albanese 7/22/13
Orson Bean............................... 7/22/28
Stephen Vincent Benet 7/22/1898
Albert Brooks........................... 7/22/47
Alexander Calder.................. 7/22/1898
George Clinton 7/22/41
Willem Dafoe........................... 7/22/55
Oscar DeLaRenta 7/22/32
Robert Dole 7/22/23
Louise Fletcher 7/22/34
Bryan Forber............................. 7/22/26
Danny Glover 7/22/47
Don Henley............................... 7/22/47
Edward Hopper 7/22/1882
Vivien Merchant 7/22/29
Tom Robbins............................. 7/22/36
Fred Roberts 7/22/62
Scott Sanderson 7/22/56
Paul Schrader 7/22/46
Terence Stamp 7/22/40
David Stieb 7/22/57
Alex Trebek............................... 7/22/40
Amy Vanderbilt 7/22/08
Margaret Whiting 7/22/28

July 23

Bert Convy 7/23/34
Gloria DeHaven 7/23/25
Don Drysdale 7/23/36
David Essex 7/23/47
James Freed 7/23/30
Woody Harrelson 7/23/61
Emil Jannings 7/23/1884
Anthony Kennedy 7/23/36
Sydney Lassick 7/23/22
Karl Menninger 7/23/1893
Belinda Montgomery 7/23/50
Alan Rafkin 7/23/28
Pee Wee Reese 7/23/18
Vincent Sardi, Jr. 7/23/15
Stephanie Seymour................... 7/23/68
Albert Warner 7/23/1884

July 24

Bella Abzug............................... 7/24/20
Peter Bart................................. 7/24/32
Barry Bonds 7/24/64
Ruth Buzzi 7/24/36
Lynda Carter............................. 7/24/51
Kenneth B. Clark 7/24/14
Amelia Earhart 7/24/1898
Steve Grogan 7/24/53
Robert Hays 7/24/47
John MacDonald 7/24/16
Karl Malone 7/24/63
Cynthia Moss............................ 7/24/40
Patrick Oliphant 7/24/35
Michael Richards 7/24/49
Billy Taylor 7/24/21
Peter Yates 7/24/29

July 25

Walter Brennan 7/25/1894
Ed Bullins 7/25/35
Frank Church............................ 7/25/24
Stanley Dancer 7/25/27
Midge Decter 7/25/27
Doug Drabek 7/25/62
Estelle Getty 7/25/24

Jack Gilford 7/25/13
Eric Hoffer 7/25/02
Iman 7/25/55
Adnan Khashoggi 7/25/35
Jim McCarty 7/25/43
Walter Payton 7/25/54
John Robinson 7/25/35
Woody Strode 7/25/14

July 26
Gracie Allen 7/26/06
Blake Edwards 7/26/22
Paul Gallico 7/26/1897
Susan George 7/26/50
Vitas Gerulitus 7/26/54
Virginia Gilmore 7/26/19
Wayne Grady 7/26/57
George Grosz 7/26/1895
Dorothy Hamill 7/26/56
Mick Jagger 7/26/43
Carl Jung 7/26/1875
Mary Jo Kopechne 7/26/40
Stanley Kubrick 7/26/28
Andre Maurois 7/26/1885
Jason Robards, Jr. 7/26/22
George Bernard Shaw 7/26/1856
Jean Shepherd 7/26/29
Kevin Spacey 7/26/59
Vivian Vance 7/26/12

July 27
Donald Crisp 7/27/1880
Irv Cross 7/27/39
Leo Durocher 7/27/06
Peggy Fleming 7/27/48
Bobby Gentry 7/27/44
Norman Lear 7/27/22
Maureen McGovern 7/27/49
Reggie McKenzie 7/27/56
Bharati Mukherjee 7/27/40
Betty Thomas 7/27/48
Jerry Van Dyke 7/27/32
Keenan Wynn 7/27/16

July 28
Mike Bloomfield 7/28/43
Vida Blue 7/28/49
Bill Bradley 7/28/43
David Brown 7/28/16
Jacques D'Amboise 7/28/34
Jim Davis 7/28/45
Marcel Duchamp 7/28/1887
Peter Duchin 7/28/37
Alberto Fujimori 7/28/38
Darryl Hickman 7/28/31
Barbara LaMarr 7/28/1896
Malcolm Lowry 7/28/09
Riccardo Muti 7/28/41
Jacqueline Onassis 7/28/29
Richard Rodgers 7/28/02
Sally Struthers 7/28/48
Rudy Vallee 7/28/01

July 29
Melvin Belli 7/29/07
Lloyd Bochner 7/29/24
Ken Burns 7/29/53
Don Carter 7/29/26
Stephen Dorff 7/29/73
Richard Egan 7/29/23
Dag Hammarskjold 7/29/05
Robert Horton 7/29/24
Peter Jennings 7/29/38
Martina McBride 7/29/66
Benito Mussolini 7/29/1883
Edwin O'Connon 7/29/18
Maria Ouspenskaya 7/29/1876
William Powell 7/29/1892
Sigmund Romberg 7/29/1887
Booth Tarkington 7/29/1869
Paul Taylor 7/29/30
Thelma Todd 7/29/05

July 30
Paul Anka 7/30/41
William Atherton 7/30/47
Peter Bogdonovich 7/30/39
Emily Bronte 7/30/1818

Delta Burke 7/30/56
Kate Bush 7/30/58
Edd Byrnes 7/30/33
Bill Cartwright 7/30/57
Larry Fishburne 7/30/61
Henry Ford 7/30/1863
Anita Hill 7/30/56
Chris Mullin 7/30/63
Ken Olin 7/30/55
Reggie Roby 7/30/61
David Sanborn 7/30/45
Patricia Schroeder 7/30/40
Arnold Schwarzenegger 7/30/47
Eleanor Smeal 7/30/39
Casey Stengel 7/30/1891

July 31

William Bennett 7/31/43
Geraldine Chaplin 7/31/44
Jean Dubuffet 7/31/01
Susan Flannery 7/31/43
Milton Friedman 7/31/12
Evonne Goolagone 7/31/51
Curt Gowdy 7/31/19
Dale Hunter 7/31/60
Stanley Jaffe 7/31/40
Irv Kupcinet 7/31/12
Sherry Lansing 7/31/44
Don Murray 7/31/29
France Nvyen 7/31/39
Wesley Snipes 7/31/62
Andre Ware 7/31/68
William Weld 7/31/45
Whitney Young 7/31/21

August 1

Tempest Bledsoe 8/1/73
Cliff Branch 8/1/48
Ron Brown 8/1/41
Robert Cray 8/1/53
Alfonse D'Amato 8/1/37
Dom Deluise 8/1/33
Jerry Garcia 8/1/42
Giancarlo Giannini 8/1/42

Arthur Hill 8/1/22
Geoffrey Holder 8/1/30
Meir Kahane 8/1/32
Robert Todd Lincoln 8/1/1843
Herman Melville 8/1/1819
Yves Saint Laurent 8/1/36
Kiki Vandeweghe 8/1/58
Jonathan Wainwright 8/1/1883
Tom Wilson 8/1/31

August 2

James Baldwin 8/2/24
Betsy Bloomingdale 8/2/26
Ann Dvorak 8/2/12
Linda Fratianne 8/2/60
Lamar Hunt 8/2/32
James Hurd 8/2/45
Lance Ito 8/2/50
Victoria Jackson 8/2/59
Aaron Krickstein 8/2/67
Paul Laxalt 8/2/22
Myrna Loy 8/2/05
Gray Merrill 8/2/15
Helen Morgan 8/2/00
Carroll O'Connor 8/2/24
Beatrice Straight 8/2/18
Peter O'Toole 8/2/33

August 3

Richard Adler 8/3/21
Tony Bennett 8/3/26
Alex Cord 8/3/31
James MacGregor Burns 8/3/18
Dolores Del Rio 8/3/05
John Eisenhower 8/3/22
John Erman 8/3/35
Jean Hagen 8/3/23
Billy James Hargis 8/3/25
Maggie Kuhn 8/3/05
John Landis 8/3/50
Marv Levy 8/3/29
Marilyn Maxwell 8/3/21
Jay North 8/3/52
Ernie Pyle 8/3/00

Martin Sheen 8/3/40
John Stennis 8/3/01
Martha Stewart 8/3/41
Leon Uris 8/3/24

August 4

Wesley Addy 8/4/13
Roger Clemens 8/4/62
Mary Decker 8/4/58
Dallas Green 8/4/34
John Riggins 8/4/49
Percy Bysshe Shelley 8/4/1792
Mary Decker Slaney 8/4/58
Helen Thomas 8/4/20
Raoul Wallenberg 8/4/12

August 5

Conrad Aiken 8/5/1889
Loni Anderson 8/5/46
Neil Armstrong 8/5/30
David Brian 8/5/14
Guy deMaupassant 8/5/1850
Tom Drake 8/5/18
Patrick Ewing 8/5/62
Roman Gabriel 8/5/40
John Huston 8/5/06
Gordon Johncock 8/5/36
Jack Kramer 8/5/21
Holly Palance 8/5/50
John Saxon 8/5/35
Jonathan Silverman 8/5/66
Erike Slezak 8/5/46
Robert Taylor 8/5/11

August 6

Lucille Ball 8/6/11
Peter Bonerz 8/6/38
Leo Carrillo 8/6/1880
Frank Finlay 8/6/26
Soleil Moon Frye 8/6/76
Hoot Gibson 8/6/1892
Helen Hull Jacob 8/6/08
Freddie Laker 8/6/22
Abbey Lincoln 8/6/30

Guthrie McClintic 8/6/1893
Robert Mitchum 8/6/17
David Robinson 8/6/65
Dutch Schultz 8/6/00
Alfred Lord Tennyson 8/6/1809
Andy Warhol 8/6/27

August 7

Ralph Bunche 8/7/04
Billie Burke 8/7/1886
Lana Cantrell 8/7/43
Rodney Crowell 8/7/50
Ada Deer 8/7/35
Edwin Edwards 8/7/27
Stan Freberg 8/7/26
Mata Hari 8/7/1876
Mickey Kantor 8/7/39
Garrison Keillor 8/7/42
Nicholas Ray 8/7/11
B.J. Thomas 8/7/42

August 8

Richard N. Anderson 8/8/26
Philip Balsley 8/8/39
Philip Barry 8/8/23
Rory Calhoun 8/8/23
Keith Carradine 8/8/49
Dino DeLaurentis 8/8/19
Arthur Goldberg 8/8/08
Matthew Henson 8/8/1866
Dustin Hoffman 8/8/37
Frank Howard 8/8/36
Joan Mondale 8/8/30
Donny Most 8/8/53
Alan Myerson 8/8/36
Deborah Norville 8/8/58
Webb Pierce 8/8/26
Marjorie Kinnan Rawlings 8/8/1896
Sylvia Sidney 8/8/10
Connie Stevens 8/8/38
Carl "Alfalfa" Switzer 8/8/26
Jerry Tarkanian 8/8/30
Mel Tillis 8/8/32
Esther Williams 8/8/23

August 9

John Cappellett	8/9/52
Bob Cousy	8/9/28
Sam Elliott	8/9/44
Charles Farrell	8/9/01
Eddy Futch	8/9/11
Leo Genn	8/9/05
Melanie Griffith	8/9/57
Ralph Houk	8/9/19
Whitney Houston	8/9/63
Burt Hull	8/9/64
Hurricane Jackson	8/9/31
Rod Laver	8/9/38
Louis Lipps	8/9/62
Kevin Mack	8/9/62
Henry Marshall	8/9/54
Ken Norton	8/9/45
Jean Piaget	8/9/1896
Deion Sanders	8/9/67
Robert Shaw	8/9/27
Ted Simmons	8/9/49
David Steinberg	8/9/42
Doug Williams	8/9/55
John "Hot Rod" Williams	8/9/61

August 10

Ian Anderson	8/10/47
Rosanna Arquette	8/10/59
Patti Austin	8/10/48
Rocky Colavito	8/10/33
Jeff Corey	8/10/14
Jimmy Dean	8/10/28
Jon Farriss	8/10/62
Eddie Fisher	8/10/28
Rhonda Fleming	8/10/23
Jack Haley	8/10/00
Red Holzman	8/10/20
Herbert Hoover	8/10/1874
Martha Hyer	8/10/24
Betsey Johnson	8/10/42
Norma Shearer	8/10/09
John Starks	8/10/65

August 11

Dik Browne	8/11/18
John Conlee	8/11/46
Arlene Dahl	8/11/27
Mike Douglas	8/11/25
Craig Ehlo	8/11/61
Rev. Jerry Falwell	8/11/33
Alex Haley	8/11/21
Clem Haskins	8/11/43
Hulk Hogan	8/11/53
Joe Jackson	8/11/55
Lloyd Noland	8/11/02
Jean Parker	8/11/12
Stuart Rosenberg	8/11/27
Carl T. Rowan	8/11/25
Otis Taylor	8/11/42
Claus Von Bulow	8/11/26

August 12

Cantinflas	8/12/11
Cecil B. DeMille	8/12/1881
John Derek	8/12/26
Samuel Fuller	8/12/12
William Goldman	8/12/31
George Hamilton	8/12/39
Parnelli Jones	8/12/33
Michael Kidd	8/12/19
Mark Knopfler	8/12/49
Norris McWhirter	8/12/25
Ross McWhirter	8/12/25
Pat Metheny	8/12/54
Buck Owens	8/12/29
John Poindexter	8/12/36
Marjorie Reynolds	8/12/21
Pete Sampras	8/12/71
Porter Wagoner	8/12/27
Jane Wyatt	8/12/12

August 13

Kathleen Battle	8/13/48
John Beal	8/13/09
Neville Brand	8/13/21
Fidel Castro	8/13/27
Joycelyn Elders	8/13/33

Dan Fogelberg	8/13/51
Pat Harrington	8/13/29
Alfred Hitchcock	8/13/1899
Don Ho	8/13/30
Ben Hogan	8/13/12
Rex Humbard	8/13/19
Bert Lahr	8/13/1895
Annie Oakley	8/13/1860
Gene Raymond	8/13/08
Buddy Rogers	8/13/04
George Shearing	8/13/19
Regis Toomey	8/13/02

August 14

Neal Anderson	8/14/64
Russell Baker	8/14/25
Halle Berry	8/14/68
John Brodie	8/14/35
David Crosby	8/14/41
John Galsworth	8/14/1867
Alice Ghostley	8/14/26
Larry Graham	8/14/46
Buddy Greco	8/14/26
Jackee	8/14/56
Ervin "Magic" Johnson	8/14/59
Arthur Laffer	8/14/35
Gary Larson	8/14/50
Steve Martin	8/14/45
Nehemiah Persoff	8/14/20
Susan Saint James	8/14/46
Danielle Steel	8/14/47
Earl Weaver	8/14/30
Lina Wertmuller	8/14/28

August 15

Princess Anne	8/15/50
Bill Baird	8/15/04
Bob Banner	8/15/21
Ethel Barrymore	8/15/1879
Robert Bolt	8/15/24
Napoleon Bonaparte	8/15/1769
Stephen Breyer	8/15/38
Peter Burns	8/15/59
Lillian Carter	8/15/1898

Julia Child	8/15/12
Samuel Taylor Coleridge	8/15/1875
Charles Comiskey	8/15/1859
Mike Connors	8/15/21
Sam Cunningham	8/15/50
Jim Dale	8/15/35
Linda Ellerbee	8/15/44
Edna Ferber	8/15/1887
Signe Hasso	8/15/15
Wendy Hiller	8/15/12
Vernon Jordan	8/15/35
Lawrence of Arabia	8/15/1888
Lori Nelson	8/15/33
Oscar Peterson	8/15/25
Nicolas Roeg	8/15/28
Phyllis Schlafly	8/15/24
Sir Walter Scott	8/15/1771
Albert Spalding	8/15/1888
Gene Upshaw	8/15/45
Jimmy Webb	8/15/46

August 16

Jimmy Arias	8/16/64
Menachem Begin	8/16/13
Bruce Beresford	8/16/40
Ann Blyth	8/16/28
Mae Clarke	8/16/07
Robert Culp	8/16/30
Suzanne Farrell	8/16/45
Tim Farris	8/16/58
Frank Gifford	8/16/30
Kathie Lee Gifford	8/16/53
Anita Gillette	8/16/36
Eydie Gorme	8/16/32
Timothy Hutton	8/16/50
Reginald Vel Johnson	8/16/52
Madonna	8/16/58
George Meany	8/16/1894
Carol Moseley-Braun	8/16/47
Julie Newmar	8/16/35
Christian Okoye	8/16/61
Fess Parker	8/16/27
Shimon Peres	8/16/23
Buck Rodgers	8/16/38

Carole Shelley 8/16/39
Glenn Strange 8/16/1899
Tony Trabert 8/16/30
Betty Von Furstenberg 8/16/31
Lesley Ann Warren 8/16/46

August 17
Richard Aldrich 8/17/02
Evelyn Ankers 8/17/20
Harve Bennett 8/17/30
Belinda Carlisle 8/17/58
Jim Courier 8/17/70
David Crockett 8/17/1786
Robert DeNiro 8/17/43
Marcus Garvey 8/17/1887
Ann Harding 8/17/04
Red Kerr 8/17/32
Christian Laettner 8/17/69
Dottie Mochrie 8/17/70
Maureen O'Hara 8/17/21
Sean Penn 8/17/60
Boog Powell 8/17/41
Francis Gary Powers 8/17/29
Marcus Roberts 8/17/63
Franklin Roosevelt, Jr. 8/17/14
Guillermo Vilas 8/17/52
Mae West.................................. 8/17/1892
Monty Woolley 8/17/1888
Jiang Zemin............................... 8/17/26

August 18
Elayne Boosler 8/18/52
Rosalynn Carter 8/18/27
Roberto Clemente 8/18/34
Marshall Field 8/18/1835
Rickey Green 8/18/54
Rafer Johnson 8/18/35
Christopher Jones 8/18/41
Alan Mowbray 8/18/1896
Martin Mull 8/18/43
Jack Pickford 8/18/1896
Roman Polanski 8/18/33
Robert Redford 8/18/37
Christian Slater 8/18/69

Patrick Swayze 8/18/52
Malcolm Jamal-Warner 8/18/70
Caspar Weinberger 8/18/17
Shelley Winters 8/18/22

August 19
Morten Anderson 8/19/60
Bernard Baruch 8/19/1870
Coco Chanel............................ 8/19/1882
Bill Clinton 8/19/46
Ron Darling 8/19/60
Claude Dauphin 8/19/03
Malcolm S. Forbes 8/19/19
Wilson Goode 8/19/38
Tipper Gore................................ 8/19/48
L.Q. Jones 8/19/27
Ring Lardner, Jr. 8/19/15
Alfred Lunt 8/19/1892
Gerald McRaney 8/19/48
Colleen Moore 8/19/02
Diana Muldaur 8/19/38
Anthony Munoz 8/19/58
Johnny Nash 8/19/40
Ogden Nash 8/19/02
Debra Paget 8/19/33
Renee Richards 8/19/34
Gene Roddenbery 8/19/21
Jill Saint John 8/19/40
Bill Shoemaker 8/19/31
John Stamos 8/19/63
Orville Wright 8/19/1871

August 20
George Aiken.......................... 8/20/1892
Joan Allen................................... 8/20/56
Macauley Caulkin 8/20/80
Connie Chung 8/20/46
Rajiv Gandhi 8/20/44
William Gray III 8/20/40
Isaac Hayes 8/20/42
H.P. Lovecraft......................... 8/20/1890
George Mitchell.......................... 8/20/33
Robert Plant 8/20/48
Regina Resnik 8/20/22

Jacqueline Susann 8/20/21
Paul Tillich 8/20/1886

August 21
Janet Baker 8/21/33
Count Basie 8/21/04
Aubrey Beardsley 8/21/1872
Wilt Chamberlain 8/21/36
Booth Gardner 8/21/36
Artis Gilmore 8/21/48
Princess Margaret 8/21/30
Patty McCormick 8/21/45
Jim McMahon 8/21/59
Kenny Rogers 8/21/38
Harry Smith 8/21/51
Melvin Van Peebles 8/21/32
Scott Williams 8/21/68

August 22
Theoni Aldredge 8/22/32
Honor Blackman 8/22/29
Ray Bradbury 8/22/20
Kathy Cennon 8/22/42
Dr. Denton Cooley 8/22/20
Morton Dean 8/22/35
Claude Debussy 8/22/1862
Malachi Favors 8/22/37
Valerie Harper 8/22/40
John Lee Hooker 8/22/17
James Kirkwood 8/22/30
Steve Kroft 8/22/45
Edgar Lee Masters 8/22/1869
Dennis McKinnon 8/22/61
Paul Molitor 8/22/56
Diana Nyad 8/22/49
Bill Parcells 8/22/41
Dorothy Parker 8/22/1893
Annie E. Proulx 8/22/35
Leni Riefenstahl 8/22/02
Diana Sands 8/22/34
Norman Schwarzkopf 8/22/34
Mats Wilander 8/22/64
Cindy Williams 8/22/47
Deng Xiaoping 8/22/04

Carl Yastrzemski 8/22/39

August 23
Tony Bill 8/23/40
Barbara Eden 8/23/34
Julio Franco 8/23/61
Sonny Jurgensen 8/23/34
George Kell 8/23/22
Gene Kelly 8/23/12
Shelley Long 8/23/49
Vera Miles 8/23/29
River Phoenix 8/23/70
Mark Russell 8/23/32
Richard Sanders 8/23/40
Rick Springfield 8/23/49
James Toney 8/23/68
Pete Wilson 8/23/33

August 24
Martine Allard 8/24/70
Yasir Arafat 8/24/29
Jorge Luis Borges 8/24/1899
Jim Capaldi 8/24/44
Gerry Cooney 8/24/56
Archie Griffin 8/24/54
Steve Guttenberg 8/24/58
Durward Kirby 8/24/12
Barry Larkin 8/24/64
Marlee Matlin 8/24/65
Reggie Miller 8/24/65
Cal Ripken, Jr. 8/24/60
Claudia Schiffer 8/24/71

August 25
Anne Archer 8/25/47
John Badham 8/25/39
Albert Bell 8/25/66
Leonard Bernstein 8/25/18
Clara Bow 8/25/05
Sean Connery 8/25/30
Elvis Costello 8/25/55
Billy Ray Cyrus 8/25/61
Don DeFore 8/25/26
Mel Ferrer 8/25/17

Rollie Finger 8/25/46
Frederick Forsyth 8/25/38
Althea Gibson 8/25/27
Monty Hall 8/25/23
Van Johnson 8/25/16
Ruby Keeler 8/25/09
Walt Kelly 8/25/13
Ted Key 8/25/12
Regis Philbin 8/25/33
Michael Rennie 8/25/09
Wayne Shoter 8/25/33
Gene Simmons 8/25/49
Tom Skerrit 8/25/33
Blair Underwood 8/25/64
Joanne Whalley-Kilmer 8/25/64
George Wallace 8/25/19

August 26
Ben Bradlee 8/26/21
Chris Burke 8/26/65
Macaulay Culkin 8/26/80
Barbara Ehrenreich 8/26/41
Geraldine Ferraro 8/26/35
Tom Heinsohohn 8/26/34
Christopher Isherwood 8/26/04
Lester Lanin 8/26/11
Irving R. Levine 8/26/22
Earl Long 8/26/1895
Bradford Marsalis 8/26/60
Brant Parker 8/26/20
Ruth Roland 8/26/1892
Albert Sabin 8/26/06
Will Shortz 8/26/52
Valerie Simpson 8/26/46
Gen. Maxwell Taylor 8/26/01
Ben Wattenberg 8/26/33

August 27
Barbara Bach 8/27/47
Alice Coltrane 8/27/37
Confucius .... 8/27/550 BC
Jeff Cook 8/27/49
Theodore Dreiser 8/27/1871
Janet Evans 8/28/71

Antonia Fraser 8/27/32
Samuel Goldwyn 8/27/1882
Georg Friedrich Hegel 8/27/1770
Pee Wee Herman 8/27/52
Lyndon Baines Johnson 8/27/08
Bob Kerry 8/27/43
Frank Leahy 8/27/08
Ira Levin 8/27/29
John Lloyd 8/27/54
Martha Raye 8/27/16
Mother Teresa 8/27/10
Tuesday Weld 8/27/43
Frank Yablans 8/27/35

August 28
Bruno Bettelheim 8/28/03
Karl Bohn 8/28/1894
Charles Boyer 8/28/1899
William Cohen 8/28/40
Marvin Davis 8/28/25
Janet Evans 8/28/71
Ben Gazzara 8/28/30
Johann Wolfgang Goethe 8/28/1749
Ron Guidry 8/28/50
Scott Hamilton 8/28/58
James Wong Howe 8/28/1899
Nancy Kulp 8/28/21
Roger Tory Peterson 8/28/08
Lou Pinella 8/28/43
Jason Priestley 8/28/69
Emma Samms 8/28/61
Tommy Sands 8/28/37
David Soul 8/28/43

August 29
Richard Attenborough 8/29/23
Carl Banks 8/29/62
Bob Beamon 8/29/46
Ingrid Bergman 8/29/16
James Brady 8/29/40
Rebecca DeMornay 8/29/62
William Friedkin 8/29/39
Elliot Gould 8/29/38
Joyce Clyde Hall 8/29/1891

Oliver Wendell Holmes 8/29/1809
Michael Jackson 8/29/58
Robin Leach 8/29/41
John Locke 8/29/1632
George Macready 8/29/09
George Montgomery 8/29/16
Charlie Parker 8/29/20
Will Perdue 8/29/65
Isabel Sanford 8/29/33
Preston Sturges 8/29/1898
Barry Sullivan 8/29/12
Dinah Washington 8/29/24

August 30

Elizabeth Ashley 8/30/39
Geoffrey Beene 8/30/27
Julie Bishop 8/30/14
Joan Blondell 8/30/12
Shirley Booth 8/30/07
Timothy Bottoms 8/30/51
Correggio 8/30/1494
Robert Crumb 8/30/43
Mickey Friedman 8/30/44
Jean-Claude Killey 8/30/43
Peggy Lipton 8/30/47
Huey P. Long 8/30/1893
Tug McGraw 8/30/44
Fred MacMurray 8/30/08
Raymond Massey 8/30/1896
Donald O'Connor 8/30/25
Robert Parish 8/30/53
Kitty Wells 8/30/19
Roy Wilkins 8/30/01
Ted Williams 8/30/18

August 31

Richard Basehart 8/31/19
Warren Berlinger 8/31/37
Marcia Clark 8/31/53
Eldridge Cleaver 8/31/35
James Coburn 8/31/28
Richard Gere 8/31/49
Debbie Gibson 8/31/70
Arthur Godfrey 8/31/03

Buddy Hackett 8/31/24
Augustus Hawkins 8/31/07
Alan Jay Lerner 8/31/18
Fredric March 8/31/1897
Maria Montessori 8/31/1870
Van Morrison 8/31/45
Hideo Nomo 8/31/68
Itzhak Perlman 8/31/45
Frank Robinson 8/31/35
William Saroyan 8/31/08
Dore Schary 8/31/05
Daniel Schorr 8/31/16
Paul Winter 8/31/39

September 1

Richard Arlen 9/1/1899
Gary Bender 9/1/40
Edgar Rice Burroughs 9/1/1875
Yvonne DeCarlo 9/1/22
Gloria Estefan 9/1/57
Richard Farnsworth 9/1/20
Vittorio Gassman 9/1/22
Barry Gibb 9/1/46
Vinnie Johnson 9/1/56
Henry Jones 9/1/12
Melvin Laird 9/1/22
George Maharis 9/1/33
Rocky Marciano 9/1/23
Dee Dee Myers 9/1/61
Seiji Ozawa 9/1/35
Walter Reuther 9/1/07
Ann Richards 9/1/33
Lily Tomlin 9/1/39
Conway Twitty 9/1/33
Don Wilson 9/1/00

September 2

Cleveland Amory 9/2/17
Nate Archibald 9/2/48
Terry Bradshaw 9/2/48
Marge Champion 9/2/23
Jimmy Connors 9/2/52
Eric Dickerson 9/2/60
Allen Drury 9/2/18

Mark Harmon 9/2/51
Martha Mitchell 9/2/18
Keanu Reeves 9/2/64
Victor Spinetti 9/2/33
John Thompson 9/2/41
Peter Ueberroth 9/2/37
Vera Vague 9/2/05

September 3
Bennie Blades 9/3/66
Eileen Brennan 9/3/37
Kitty Carlisle 9/3/15
Pauline Collins 9/3/40
Natalie Fuchs 9/3/52
Anne Jackson 9/3/26
Al Jardine 9/3/42
Burt Kennedy 9/3/22
Alan Ladd 9/3/13
Alison Lurie 9/3/26
Irene Papas 9/3/26
Valerie Perrine 9/3/43
George Pirkle 9/3/47
Charlie Sheen 9/3/65
Bob Ussery 9/3/35
Mort Walker 9/3/23

September 4
Nigel Bruce 9/4/1895
Richard Castellano 9/4/34
Edward Dmytryk 9/4/08
Thomas Eagleton 9/4/29
Henry Ford II 9/4/17
Mitzi Gaynor 9/4/31
Paul Harvey 9/4/18
Judith Ivey 9/4/51
Ida Kaminska 9/4/1899
Jennifer Salt 9/4/44
Tom Watson 9/4/49
Richard Wright 9/4/08
Dick York 9/4/28

September 5
John Cage 9/5/12
Morris Carnovsky 9/5/1897

John Danforth 9/5/36
William Devane 9/5/39
Florence Eldridge 9/5/01
Werner Erhard 9/5/35
Willie Gault 9/5/60
Cathy Guisewite 9/5/50
Alcee Hastings 9/5/36
Jesse James 9/5/1847
Billy Kilmer 9/5/39
Carol Lawrence 9/5/32
Buddy Miles 9/5/46
John Mitchell 9/5/13
Bob Newhart 9/5/29
Arthur C. Nielsen 9/5/1897
Jack Valenti 9/5/21
Paul Volcker 9/5/27
Racquel Welch 9/5/40
Barry Williams 9/5/54
Frank Yerby 9/5/16
Darryl F. Zanuck 9/5/02

September 6
Mark Chestnutt 9/6/63
David Allen Coe 9/6/39
Jane Curtin 9/6/47
Werner Herzog 9/6/42
Joseph Kennedy 9/6/1888
Otto Kruger 9/6/1885
Swoosie Kurtz 9/6/44
Mel McDaniel 9/6/42
Billy Rose 9/6/1899
Jo Anne Worley 9/6/37

September 7
Corbin Bernsen 9/7/54
Susan Blakely 9/7/48
Paul Brown 9/7/08
Taylor Caldwell 9/7/00
Dr. Michael DeBakery 9/7/08
Michael Feinstein 9/7/56
Gloria Gaynor 9/7/48
Giuseppe Giacomini 9/7/40
Samuel Goldwyn, Jr. 9/7/26
Grandma Moses 9/7/1860

Buddy Holly 9/7/36
Chrissie Hynde 9/7/57
Daniel Inouye 9/7/24
Julie Kavner 9/7/51
Elia Kazan 9/7/09
John Phillip Law 9/7/37
Peter Lawford 9/7/23
Peggy Noonan 9/7/50
Anthony Quayle 9/7/13
Sonny Rollins 9/7/30
Richard Roundtree 9/7/42
Al Sherman 9/7/1897
Susan Stamberg 9/7/38
Jerry Zaks 9/7/46

September 8
Ann Beattie 9/8/47
William Bligh 9/8/1754
Hillary Brooke 9/8/16
Sid Caesar 9/8/22
Stefano Casiraghi 9/8/60
Maurice Cheeks 9/8/56
Patsy Cline 9/8/32
Denise Darcel 9/8/25
Howard Dietz 9/8/1896
Euell Gibbons 9/8/11
Ron McKernan 9/8/46
Freddie Mercury 9/8/46
Grace Metalious 9/8/24
Sam Nunn 9/8/38
Claude Pepper 9/8/00
Richard the Loin Hearted 9/8/1157
Peter Sellers 9/8/25
Larenz Tate 9/8/75
Heather Thomas 9/8/57

September 9
B.J. Armstrong 9/9/67
John Curry 9/9/49
Arthur Freed 9/9/1894
Jane Greer 9/9/24
Hugh Grant 9/9/60
Michael Keaton 9/9/51
Joseph Levine 9/9/05

Dan Majerle 9/9/65
Kristy McNichol 9/9/62
Sylvia Miles 9/9/32
Billy Preston 9/9/46
Otis Redding 9/9/41
Cliff Robertson 9/9/25
Col. Harland Sanders 9/9/1890
Joe Theismann 9/9/49
Leo Tolstoy 9/9/1828
Tom Wopat 9/9/52

September 10
John Entwistle 9/10/44
Jose Feliciano 9/10/45
Stephen Jay Gould 9/10/41
Amy Irving 9/10/53
Charles Kuralt 9/10/34
Karl Lagerfeld 9/10/38
Bob Lanier 9/10/48
Bessie Love 9/10/1898
Roger Maris 9/10/34
Edmund O'Brien 9/10/15
Arnold Palmer 9/10/29
Irwin Rosten 9/10/24
Yma Sumac 9/10/27
Sedale Threatt 9/10/61
Robert Wise 9/10/14

September 11
Sarah Bache 9/11/1744
David Broder 9/11/29
Kevin Brophy 9/11/53
Paul "Bear" Bryant 9/11/13
Harry Connick, Jr. 9/11/67
Brian Depalma 9/11/40
Charles Evers 9/11/22
Lola Falana 9/11/43
Henderson Forsythe 9/11/17
Mickey Hart 9/11/43
O. Henry 9/11/1862
Earl Holliman 9/11/20
Ramez Idriss 9/11/11
Tom Landry 9/11/24
D.H. Lawrence 9/11/1885

Ferdinand Marcos 9/11/17
Bob Packwood 9/11/32
Arvo Part 9/11/35
Gerald Wilkins 9/11/63

September 12
Ki-Jana Carter 9/12/73
Maurice Chevalier 9/12/1888
Irene Dailey 9/12/20
Gunther Gebel-Williams 9/12/34
Linda Gray 9/12/41
Tim Haraway 9/12/66
Ian Holm 9/12/31
George Jones 9/12/31
Alfred A. Knopf 9/12/1892
H.L. Mencken 9/12/1880
Dickie Moore 9/12/25
Maria Muldaur 9/12/43
Jesse Owens 9/12/13
Peter Scolari 9/12/54
Stephen Solarz 9/12/40
Valadimir Spivakov 9/12/44
Tatiana Troyanos 9/12/38
Barry White 9/12/44

September 13
Barbara Bain 9/13/32
Jacqueline Bisset 9/13/44
Scott Brady 9/13/24
Nell Carter 9/13/48
Claudette Colbert 9/13/05
Roald Dahl 9/13/16
Dick Haymes 9/13/17
Leland Hayward 9/13/02
Milton Hershey 9/13/1857
Maurice Jarre 9/13/24
Jesse Lasky 9/13/1880
Judith Martin 9/13/38
Mae Questel 9/13/08
Walter Reed 9/13/1851
Arnold Schoenberg 9/13/1874
Mel Torme 9/13/25

September 14

Larry Brown 9/14/40
Zoe Caldwell 9/14/33
Mary Crosby 9/14/59
Faith Ford 9/14/64
Raymond Floyd 9/14/42
Jack Hawkins 9/14/10
Joey Heatherton 9/14/44
Clayton Moore 9/14/14
Joe Penny 9/14/56
Margaret Sanger 9/14/1883
Van Gordon Sauter 9/14/35
Nicol Williams 9/14/38

September 15
Creighton Abrams 9/15/44
Roy Acuff 9/15/03
"Cannonball" Adderley 9/15/28
Robert Benchley 9/15/1889
Agatha Christie 9/15/1890
Jackie Cooper 9/15/22
James Fenimore Cooper 9/15/1789
Norm Crosby 9/15/27
Tommy Lee Jones 9/15/46
Alexander Korda 9/15/1893
Margaret Lockwood 9/15/16
Dan Marino 9/15/61
Chris Menge 9/15/40
Pete Myers 9/15/63
Jessye Norman 9/15/45
Merlin Olsen 9/15/40
Gaylord Perry 9/15/38
Jean Renoir 9/15/1894
Bobby Short 9/15/24
Penny Singleton 9/15/08
Oliver Stone 9/15/46
William Howard Taft 9/15/1857
Bruno Walter 9/15/1876
Fay Wray 9/15/07

September 16
Lauren Bacall 9/16/24
Elgin Baylor 9/16/34
Ed Begley, Jr. 9/16/49
Charles Byrd 9/16/25

Rosemary Casals 9/16/48
George Chakiris 9/16/34
David Copperfield 9/16/56
Peter Falk 9/16/27
Anne Francis 9/16/30
Allen Funt 9/16/14
Orel Hershiser 9/16/58
B.B. King 9/16/25
Lee Kuan Yee 9/16/23
Janis Paige 9/16/22
Jerry Pate 9/16/53
J.C. Penny 9/16/1875
Tim Rains 9/16/59
Susan Ruttan 9/16/48
Robert Schuller 9/16/26
Mickey Tettleton 9/16/60
Jerry Wald 9/16/11
Thomas Woodward 9/16/25
Lee Kuan Yew 9/16/23
Robin Yount 9/16/55

September 17

Anne Bancroft 9/17/31
George Blanda 9/17/27
Warren Burger 9/17/07
Anthony Carter 9/17/60
Orlando Cepeda 9/17/37
Dolores Costello 9/17/05
Patricia Crowley 9/17/38
David Huddleston 9/17/30
Phil Jackson 9/17/45
Kent Kesey 9/17/35
Dorothy Loudon 9/17/33
Jeffrey MacNelly 9/17/47
John W. Marriott 9/17/00
Robert Matsui 9/17/47
Roddy McDowell 9/17/28
Stirling Moss 9/17/29
Robert Brown Parker 9/17/32
John Ritter 9/17/48
David Souter 9/17/39
Ben Turpin 9/17/1874
Hank Williams 9/17/23

September 18

Eddie Anderson 9/18/05
Leon Askin 9/18/07
Frankie Avalon 9/18/40
Chip Banks 9/18/59
Robert Blakes 9/18/33
Scotty Bowman 9/18/33
Rossano Brazzi 9/18/16
Agnes DeMille 9/18/05
Greta Garbo 9/18/05
Dennis Johnson 9/18/54
Samuel Johnson 9/18/1709
Phyllis Kirk 9/18/29
Toni Kukoc 9/18/68
Richard Pitino 9/18/52
Holly Robinson 9/18/64
Ryne Sandberg 9/18/59
Billy Sims 9/18/55
Anna Dearee Smith 9/18/50
Jack Warden 9/18/20

September 19

Jim Abbott 9/19/67
Jane Blalock 9/19/45
Ricardo Cortez 9/19/1899
Cass Elliot 9/19/43
Frances Farmer 9/19/13
William Golding 9/19/11
Michael Greer 9/19/17
Dan Hampton 9/19/57
Rosemary Harris 9/19/30
Jeremy Irons 9/19/48
Joan Lunden 9/19/51
Randolph Mantooth 9/19/44
David McCallum 9/19/33
Nat Moore 9/19/51
Joe Morgan (Baseball Player) .. 9/19/43
Joseph Pasternak 9/19/01
Freda Payne 9/19/45
Lewis Powell, Jr. 9/19/07
Mike Royko 9/19/32
Duke Snider 9/19/26
Twiggy 9/19/49
Trisha Yearwood 9/19/64

Adam West 9/19/28
Paul Williams 9/19/40

September 20
Alexander the Great .... 9/20/356 BC
Red Auerbach 9/20/17
Crispin Glover 9/20/64
Guy Lafleur 9/20/51
Pia Lindstrom 9/20/38
Sophia Loren 9/20/34
Anne Meara 9/20/29
Jelly Roll Morton 9/20/1885
Fernando Rey 9/20/17
Rachel Roberts 9/20/27
Upton Sinclair 9/20/1818
Jim Taylor 9/20/35

September 21
Dawn Addams 9/21/30
John Bunny 9/21/1863
Dave Coulier 9/21/59
D.J. Dozier 9/21/65
Ladislas Farago 9/21/06
Cecil Fielder 9/21/63
Henry Gibson 9/21/35
Larry Hagman 9/21/31
Hamilton Jordan 9/21/44
Stephen King 9/21/47
John Kluge 9/21/14
Bill Kurtis 9/21/40
Ricki Lake 9/21/68
Rick Mahorn 9/21/58
Doug Moe 9/21/38
Sidney Moncrief 9/21/57
Bill Murray 9/21/50
Gail Russell 9/21/24
H. G. Wells 9/21/1866

September 22
Scott Baio 9/22/61
Shari Belafonte 9/22/54
Debbie Boone 9/22/56
John Houseman 9/22/02
Joan Jett 9/22/59

Ingemar Johansson 9/22/32
Tommy Lasorda 9/22/27
Bob Lemon 9/22/20
Paul Muni 9/22/1895
Catherine Oxenberg 9/22/61
Martha Scott 9/22/14
David Stern 9/22/42
Erich Von Stroheim 9/22/1885

September 23
Jason Alexander 9/23/59
Roy Buchanan 9/23/39
Ray Charles 9/23/30
John Coltrane 9/23/26
Julio Iglesias 9/23/43
Stanley Kramer 9/23/13
Walter Pidgeon 9/23/1897
Mickey Rooney 9/23/20
Romy Schneider 9/23/38
Martin Schottenhheimer 9/23/43
Bruce Springsteen 9/23/49
George Wolfe 9/23/54

September 24
Hollis Alpert 9/24/16
F. Scott Fitzgerald 9/24/1896
Larry Gates 9/24/15
"Mean" Joe Green 9/24/46
Jim Henson 9/24/36
Patrick Kelly 9/24/54
Joseph P. Kennedy 9/24/52
Sheila MacRae 9/24/24
Linda McCartney 9/24/42
Jim McKay 9/24/21
Anthony Newley 9/24/31

September 25
Michael Douglas 9/25/44
John Ericson 9/25/26
Max Factor III 9/25/45
William Faulkner 9/25/1897
Robert Gates 9/25/43
Glenn Gould 9/25/32
Mark Hamill 9/25/51

Daniel W. Hillis 9/25/56
Bell Hooks 9/25/52
Heather Locklear 9/25/61
Bob McAdoo 9/25/51
Scottie Pippen 9/25/65
Juliet Prowse 9/25/36
Aldo Ray 9/25/26
Christopher Reeve 9/25/52
Phil Rizzuto 9/25/18
Mark Rothko 9/25/03
Dmitri Shostakovich 9/25/06
Red Smith 9/25/05
Wil Smith 9/25/68
Cheryl Tiegs 9/25/47
Robert Walden 9/25/43
Barbara Walters 9/25/31
Anson Williams 9/25/49

September 26
Lynn Anderson 9/26/47
Melissa Sue Anderson 9/26/62
Johnny Appleseed 9/26/1774
Philip Michael Bosco 9/26/30
Barbara Britton 9/26/19
Andrea Dworkin 9/26/46
T.S. Eliot 9/26/1888
Bryan Ferry 9/26/45
George Gershwin 9/26/1898
Linda Hamilton 9/26/57
Mary Beth Hurt 9/26/48
Jack LaLanne 9/26/14
Lawrence Leritz 9/26/52
Julie London 9/26/26
Olivia Newton-John 9/26/48
Patrick O'Neal 9/26/27
George Raft 9/26/1895
Marty Robbins 9/26/25

September 27
Samuel Adams 9/27/1722
Louis Auchincloss 9/27/17
Wilford Brimley 9/27/34
Shaun Cassidy 9/27/58
William Conrad 9/27/20a

Don Cornelius 9/27/36
Misha Dichter 9/27/45
Sam Ervin 9/27/1896
Betty Howar 9/27/34
Claude Jarman, Jr. 9/27/34
Steve Kerr 9/27/65
Jayne Meadows 9/27/26
Meat Loaf 9/27/48
Greg Morris 9/27/34
Kathleen Nolan 9/27/33
Arthur Penn 9/27/22
Charles Percy 9/27/19
Mike Schmidt 9/27/49
Sada Thompson 9/27/29
Heather Watts 9/27/43
Kathrynne Whitworth 9/27/39

September 28
Brigitte Bardot 9/28/34
Al Capp 9/28/09
Peter Finch 9/28/16
Janice Hall 9/28/53
Ben E. King 9/28/38
Steve Largent 9/28/54
Marcello Mastroianni 9/28/24
William Paley 9/28/01
Elmer Rice 9/28/1892
Ethel Rosenberg 9/28/15
John Sayles 9/28/50
Max Schmeling 9/28/05
Ed Sullivan 9/28/02
William Windom 9/28/23

September 29
Michelangelo Antonioni 9/29/12
Gene Autry 9/29/07
Virginia Bruce 9/29/10
Miguel de Cervantes 9/29/1547
Sebastian Coe 9/29/56
Anita Ekberg 9/29/31
Enrico Fermi 9/29/01
Mike Frankovich 9/29/10
Greer Garson 9/29/08
Bryant Gumbel 9/29/48

Hersey Hawkins 9/29/66
Trevor Howard 9/29/16
Madeline Kahn 9/29/42
Jerry Lee Lewis 9/29/35
Larry Linville 9/29/39
Paul McCloskey 9/29/27
Ken Norton, Jr. 9/29/66
John Paxson 9/29/60
Lizabeth Scott 9/29/22
Lech Walesa 9/29/43
Jill Whelan 9/29/66

September 30
Renee Adoree 9/30/1898
Deborah Allen 9/30/53
Kenny Baker 9/30/12
Truman Capote 9/30/24
Len Carion 9/30/39
Angie Dickinson 9/30/31
Deborah Kerr 9/30/21
Lester Maddox 9/30/15
Johnny Mathis 9/30/35
Marilyn McCoo 9/30/44
Jody Powell 9/30/43
Eric Stoltz 9/30/61
Marty Stuart 9/30/58
Elie Wiesel 9/30/28

October 1
Julie Andrews 10/1/35
Tom Bosley 10/1/27
Rod Carew 10/1/45
Jimmy Carter 10/1/24
Stephen Collins 10/1/47
George Coulouris 10/1/03
Hiram Fong 10/1/07
Richard Harris 10/1/33
Laurence Harvey 10/1/28
Stanley Holloway 10/1/1890
Vladimir Horowitz 10/1/04
Fletcher Knebel 10/1/11
Walter Matthau 10/1/20
Mary McFadden 10/1/38
Youssou Ndour 10/1/59

George Peppard 10/1/28
William Rehnquist 10/1/24
Everett Sloane 10/1/09
Stella Stevens 10/1/36
Wallace Stevens 10/1/1879
Edward Villella 10/1/32
James Whitmore 10/1/21
Sam Yorty 10/1/09

October 2
William "Budd" Abbott 10/2/00
Johnnie Cochran, Jr 10/2/37
Mahatma Gandhi 10/2/1869
Graham Green 10/2/04
Moses Gunn 10/2/29
Donna Karan 10/2/48
Persis Khambata 10/2/50
Spanky MacFarland 10/2/28
"Groucho" Marx 10/2/1890
Don McLean 10/2/45
Jana Novotna 10/2/68
Alex Raymond 10/2/09
Rex Reed 10/2/40
Richard III 10/2/1452
Sting 10/2/51
Nat Turner 10/2/1800
Maury Wills 10/2/32

October 3
Gertrude Berg 10/3/1899
Hart Bochner 10/3/56
Lindsey Buckingham 10/3/49
Chubby Checker 10/3/41
Fred Couples 10/3/59
Dennis Eckersley 10/3/54
James Herriot 10/3/16
Harvey Kurtzman 10/3/24
Tommy Lee 10/3/62
John MacLeod 10/3/37
Leo McCarey 10/3/1898
Warner Oland 10/3/1880
Madlyn Rhue 10/3/34
Gore Vidal 10/3/25
Jack Wagner 10/3/59

Dave Winfield 10/3/51
Thomas Wolfe 10/3/00

October 4

Armand Assante 10/4/49
Jackie Collins 10/4/41
Clifton Davis 10/4/45
Brenda Gill 10/4/14
A.C. Green 10/4/63
Rutherford B. Hayes 10/4/1822
Charlton Heston 10/4/24
Sam Huff 10/4/34
Buster Keaton 10/4/1896
Tony Larussa 10/4/44
Jan Murray 10/4/17
Michael Pare 10/4/59
Frederic Remington 10/4/1861
Anne Rice 10/4/41
Damon Runyon 10/4/1884
Susan Sarandon 10/4/46
Alvin Toffler 10/4/28

October 5

Peter Ackroyd 10/5/49
Karen Allen 10/5/51
Clive Barker 10/5/52
Diane Cilento 10/5/33
Jeff Conaway 10/5/50
Bill Dana 10/5/24
Larry Fine 10/5/02
Eugene Fodor (publisher) 10/5/14
Bob Geldof 10/5/51
Vaclav Havel 10/5/36
Grant Hill 10/5/72
Skip Homeier 10/5/30
Glynis Johns 10/5/23
Ray Kroc 10/5/02
Mario Lemieux 10/5/65
Maya Lin 10/5/59
Joshua Logan 10/5/08
Steve Miller 10/5/43
Donald Pleasence 10/5/19
Elke Sommer 10/5/40
Barry Switzer 10/5/37

Robert Trout 10/5/08

October 6

Gerry Adams 10/6/48
Shana Alexander 10/6/25
Hafez al Assad 10/6/30
Jerome Cowan 10/6/1897
Britt Ekland 10/6/42
Janet Gaynor 10/6/06
Thor Heyerdahl 10/6/14
Meyer Levin 10/6/05
Carol Lombard 10/6/09
Napoleon McCallum 10/6/63
Anna Quayle 10/6/36
Jack Sharkey 10/6/02
Ruben Sierra 10/6/65
Lowell Thomas, Jr. 10/6/23
Fred Travalena 10/6/43
Stephaine Zimbalist 10/6/56

October 7

June Allyson 10/7/17
Niels Bohr 10/7/1895
Toni Braxton 10/7/67
Sarah Churchill 10/7/14
Gabe Dell 10/7/23
Andy Devine 10/7/05
Alfred Drake 10/7/14
Charles Dutoit 10/7/36
Ellaraino 10/7/38
Cotton Fitzsimmons 10/7/31
Heinrich Himmler 10/7/00
Elizabeth Janeway 10/7/13
Leroi Jones 10/7/34
R.D. Laing 10/7/27
Diana Lynn 10/7/26
Yo-Yo Ma 10/7/55
Uncle Dave Macon 10/7/1870
John Cougar Mellcamp 10/7/51
Vaughn Monroe 10/7/11
Elijah Muhammad 10/7/1897
Oliver North 10/7/43
Reid Shelton 10/7/24
Reggie Smythe 10/7/17

Bishop Desmond Tutu 10/7/31

October 8
Jorge Amado 10/8/12
Rona Barrett 10/8/36
Matt Bionde 10/8/65
Chevy Chase 10/8/43
Bill Elliott 10/8/55
Jesse Jackson 10/8/41
Gus Hall 10/8/10
Juan Peron 10/8/1895
Eddie Rickenbacker 10/8/1890
Faith Ringgold 10/8/30
Sigourney Weaver 10/8/49

October 9
Kenny Anderson 10/9/70
Edward Andrews 10/9/14
Jackson Browne 10/9/50
Bruce Catton 10/9/1899
Gary Frank 10/9/50
E. Howard Hunt 10/9/18
Brian Lamb 10/9/41
John Lennon 10/9/40
Sean Lennon 10/9/75
Trent Lott 10/9/41
Aimee Semple McPherson .. 10/9/1890
Russell Myers 10/9/38
Alistair Sim 10/9/00
Mike Singletary 10/9/58
Jacques Tati 10/9/08
Robert Wuhl 10/9/51

October 10
James Clavell 10/10/24
Vernon Duke 10/10/03
Brett Favre 10/10/69
Helen Hayes 10/10/00
Keith Hernandez 10/10/53
Richard Jaeckel 10/10/30
Johnny Marks 10/10/09
Thelonious Monk 10/10/20
Sir Harold Pinter 10/10/30
John Prine 10/10/46

David Lee Roth 10/10/55
Omar Sharif 10/10/32
Claude Simon 10/10/13
John Studebaker 10/10/1833
Tanya Tucker 10/10/58
Giuseppe Verdi 10/10/1813
Ben Vereen 10/10/46

October 11
Joseph Alsop 10/11/10
Art Blakey 10/11/19
Norm Cash 10/11/34
Joan Cusack 10/11/62
Daryl Hall 10/11/48
Henry J. Heinz 10/11/1844
Earle Hyman 10/11/26
Ron Leibman 10/11/37
Elmore Leonard 10/11/25
Peter Martins 10/11/46
Patty Murray 10/11/50
Norm Nixon 10/11/55
Luke Perry 10/11/65
William J. Perry 10/11/27
Charles Revson 10/11/06
Jerome Robbins 10/11/16
Eleanor Roosevelt 10/11/1884
Charles Shyer 10/11/41
Chris Spielman 10/11/65
Steve Young 10/11/61

October 12
Kirk Cameron 10/12/70
Dick Gregory 10/12/32
Tony Kubek 10/12/35
Sam Moore 10/12/35
Jean Nidetch 10/12/23
Luciano Pavarotti 10/12/35
Richard Price 10/12/49
Adam Rich 10/12/68
Chris Wallace 10/12/47

October 13
Lenny Bruce 10/13/25
Shirley Caesar 10/13/38

Tisha Campbell 10/13/70
Laraine Day 10/13/20
Art Garfunkel 10/13/42
Frank Gilroy 10/13/25
Sammy Hagar 10/13/49
Derek Harper 10/13/61
Herblock 10/13/09
Beverly Johnson 10/13/52
Nancy Kerrigan 10/13/69
Rich Kottite 10/13/42
Jack MacGowran 10/13/18
Yves Montand 10/13/21
Marie Osmond 10/13/59
Kelly Preston 10/13/62
Jerry Rice 10/13/62
Irene Rich 10/13/1891
Doc Rivers 10/13/61
Nipsy Russell 10/13/24
Paul Simon 10/13/41
Art Tatum 10/13/10
Margaret Thatcher 10/13/25
Pamela Tiffin 10/13/42
Burr Tillstrom 10/13/17
Cornel Wilde 10/13/18
Desmond Wilson 10/13/46

October 14
Harry Anderson 10/14/52
Keith Byars 10/14/63
E.E. Cummings 10/14/1894
Beth Daniel 10/14/56
John Dean 10/14/38
Dwight Eisenhower 10/14/1890
Greg Evigan 10/14/53
Lillian Gish 10/14/1896
Jerry Glanville 10/14/41
Allan Jones 10/14/07
Ralph Lauren 10/14/39
Roger Moore 10/14/27
J.C. Snead 10/14/41
Karyn White 10/14/64
John Wooden 10/14/10

October 15
Boris Aronson 10/15/00
Chuck Berry 10/15/26
Richard Carpenter 10/15/46
Ina Claire 10/15/1895
Jane Darwell 10/15/1880
Fritz Feld 10/15/00
Sarah Ferguson 10/15/59
John Kenneth Galbraith 10/15/08
Peter Haskell 10/15/34
Evan Hunter 10/15/26
Lee Iacocca 10/15/24
Tito Jackson 10/15/53
Linda Lavin 10/15/37
Mervyn LeRoy 10/15/00
Penny Marshall 10/15/45
William Menninger 10/15/1899
Friedrich Nietzsche 10/15/1844
Jim Palmer 10/15/45
Jean Peters 10/15/26
Mario Puzo 10/15/20
Arthur Schlesinger, Jr. 10/15/17
Roscoe Tanner 10/15/51
Virgil .... 10/15/70 BC

October 16
Rex Bell 10/16/05
David Ben-Gurion 10/16/1886
Manute Bol 10/16/62
Linda Darnell 10/16/21
Dave Debusschere 10/16/40
Chris Doleman 10/16/61
Gunter Grass 10/16/27
C. Everett Koop 10/16/16
Angela Lansbury 10/16/25
Tim McCarver 10/16/41
Eugene O'Neill 10/16/1888
Tim Robbins 10/16/58
Suzanne Somers 10/16/46
Noah Webster 10/16/1758
Oscar Wilde 10/16/1856
Kathleen Winsor 10/16/16
David Zucker 10/16/47

October 17

Julia Adams	10/17/28
Jean Arthur	10/17/09
Jimmy Breslin	10/17/30
Spring Byington	10/17/1893
Montgomery Cliff	10/17/20
Danny Ferry	10/17/66
Rita Hayworth	10/17/18
Marsha Hunt	10/17/17
Alan Jackson	10/17/58
Mae Jemison	10/17/56
Margot Kidder	10/17/48
Evel Knievel	10/17/39
Dolph Lundgren	10/17/59
Arthur Miller	10/17/15
Vincent Van Patten	10/17/57
Tom Poston	10/17/27
Howard Rollins	10/17/50
Irene Ryan	10/17/03
George Wendt	10/17/48
Nathanael West	10/17/03

October 18

Peter Boyle	10/18/35
Leo G. Carroll	10/18/1892
Violeta Chamarro	10/18/29
Pam Dawber	10/18/51
Mike Ditka	10/18/39
Forrest Gregg	10/18/33
Tommy Hearns	10/18/58
Jesse Helms	10/18/21
Miriam Hopkins	10/18/02
Willie Horton (Baseball)	10/18/42
Keith Jackson	10/18/28
Sidney Kingsley	10/18/06
Lotte Lenya	10/18/00
Wynton Marsalis	10/18/61
Melina Mercouri	10/18/25
Erin Moran	10/18/61
Martina Navatilova	10/18/56
Laura Nyro	10/18/47
Anita O'Day	10/18/18
Lee Harvey Oswald	10/18/39

George C. Scott	10/18/27
Ntozake Shange	10/18/48
Inger Stevens	10/18/34
Pierre Trudeau	10/18/19

October 19

Renata Adler	10/19/38
Jack Anderson	10/19/22
Richard Arrington	10/19/34
Robert Beatty	10/19/09
Umberto Boccioni	10/19/1882
Amy Carter	10/19/67
Brad Daugherty	10/19/65
Sean Garrison	10/19/37
Jennifer Holliday	10/19/60
Evander Holyfield	10/19/62
John LeCarre	10/19/31
John Lithgow	10/19/45
Peter Max	10/19/37
Robert Reed	10/19/32
Jeannie C. Riley	10/19/45
Louis Scheimer	10/19/28
Robert Strauss	10/19/18

October 20

Dr. Joyce Brothers	10/20/28
Art Buchwald	10/20/25
Barrie Chase	10/20/34
John Dewey	10/20/1859
Margaret Dumont	10/20/1889
Arlene Francis	10/20/08
Charles Ives	10/20/1874
Bela Lugosi	10/20/1882
Mickey Mantle	10/20/31
Melanie Mayron	10/20/52
Fayard Antonio Nichlas	10/20/14
Jerry Orbach	10/20/35
Tom Petty	10/20/52
Ellery Queen	10/20/05
Ray Rhodes	10/20/52
Eric Scott	10/20/58

October 21

Carrie Fisher	10/21/56
Whitey Ford	10/21/28
Dizzy Gillespie	10/21/17
Mike Keenan	10/21/49
Ursula LeGuin	10/21/29
Manfred Mann	10/21/40
Jeremy Miller	10/21/76
Jan Morris	10/21/26
Alfred Bernhard Nobel	10/21/1833
Mark Rypien	10/21/62
Sir George Solti	10/21/12
Julie Wilson	10/21/24

October 22

Constance Bennett	10/22/05
Brian Boitano	10/22/63
Catherine Deneuve	10/22/43
Joan Fontaine	10/22/17
Jimmy Fox	10/22/07
Annette Funicello	10/22/42
Jeff Goldblum	10/22/52
Curly Howard	10/22/03
Derek Jacobi	10/22/38
Alan Ladd, Jr.	10/22/37
Timothy Leary	10/22/20
Doris Lessing	10/22/19
Christopher Lloyd	10/22/38
William Morris, Jr.	10/22/1899
Robert Rauschenberg	10/22/25
Tony Roberts	10/22/39
Bobby Seale	10/22/37
N.C. Wyeth	10/22/1882

October 23

Sarah Bernhardt	10/23/1844
Jim Bunning	10/23/31
Johnny Carson	10/23/25
Michael Crichton	10/23/42
James Daly	10/23/18
Bella Darvi	10/23/29
Diana Dors	10/23/31
John W. Heisman	10/23/1869
Phil Kaufman	10/23/36
Bob Montana	10/23/20
Pele	10/23/40
Chi Chi Rodriguez	10/23/35
Ned Rorem	10/23/23
Weird Al Yankovic	10/23/59
Dwight Yoakam	10/23/56

October 24

F. Murray Abraham	10/24/39
Jackie Coogan	10/24/14
Preston Foster	10/24/02
Moss Hart	10/24/04
Bob Kane	10/24/16
Kevin Kline	10/24/47
Ted Lewis	10/24/1894
Juan Marichal	10/24/37
Kweisi Mfume	10/24/48
David Nelson	10/24/36
Jay Novacek	10/24/62
Cheryl Studer	10/24/55
Y.A. Tittle	10/24/26
Tony Walton	10/24/34
David Ward	10/24/47
B.D. Wong	10/24/62
William Wyman	10/24/41

October 25

John Berryman	10/25/14
George Bizet	10/25/1838
James Carville	10/25/44
Henry Steel Commager	10/25/02
Barbara Cook	10/25/27
Dave Cowens	10/25/48
John Francis Dodge	10/25/1864
Dan Issel	10/25/48
Bobby Knight	10/25/40
Minnie Pearl	10/25/12
Pablo Picasso	10/25/1881
Helen Reddy	10/25/41
Marion Ross	10/25/28
Steve Shagan	10/25/27
Johann Strauss, Jr.	10/25/1825
Pat Swilling	10/25/64

October 26

Edward Brooke 10/26/19
Primo Carnera 10/26/06
Hillary Rodham Clinton 10/26/47
Pat Conroy 10/26/45
Cary Elwes 10/26/62
Bob Hoskins 10/26/42
Mahalia Jackson 10/26/11
John Knight 10/26/1894
Marla Maples-Trump 10/26/63
Francois Mitterrand 10/26/16
Shelly Morrison 10/26/36
Shah Reza Pahlavi 10/26/19
Pat Sajak 10/26/46
Julian Schnabel 10/26/51
Jaclyn Smith 10/26/47

October 27

Michael Angelo Avallone 10/27/24
Jack Carson 10/27/10
Warren Christopher 10/27/25
John Cleese.............................. 10/27/39
Fred DeCordova 10/27/10
Ruby Dee................................. 10/27/24
Jeff East.................................... 10/27/57
Leif Erikson............................. 10/27/11
Nanette Fabray 10/27/22
Lee Greenwood 10/27/42
H.R. Haldeman 10/27/26
Jayne Kennedy-Overton 10/27/51
Simon Le Bon........................... 10/27/58
Fran Lebowitz 10/27/50
Roy Lichtenstein 10/27/23
Peter Marten 10/27/46
Sylvia Plath 10/27/32
Ivan Reitman 10/27/46
Theodore Roosevelt 10/27/1858
Isaac Singer 10/27/1811
Carrie Snodgress 10/27/46
Oliver Tambo........................... 10/27/17
Dylan Thomas 10/27/14
Teresa Wright 10/27/18

October 28

Jane Alexander 10/28/39
Stephen Atwater 10/28/66
Francis Bacon.......................... 10/28/10
Charlie Daniel......................... 10/28/36
Tony Franciosa 10/28/28
Dennis Franz 10/28/44
William "Bill" Gates 10/28/55
Edith Head 10/28/07
Telma Hopkins 10/28/48
Bruce Jenner............................ 10/28/49
Bowie Kuhn 10/28/26
Cleo Laine 10/28/27
Elsa Lancaster 10/28/02
Suzy Parker............................. 10/28/33
Joan Plowright......................... 10/28/29
Annie Potts 10/28/52
Julia Roberts............................ 10/28/67
Jonas Salk 10/28/14
Evelyn Waugh 10/28/03
Lenny Wilkens 10/28/37

October 29

James Boswell 10/29/1740
Fanny Brice 10/29/1891
Geraldine Brooks 10/29/25
Richard Dreyfuss 10/29/47
Kate Jackson 10/29/49
Connie Mack........................... 10/29/40
Bill Mauldin 10/29/21
Melba Moore 10/29/45
Winona Ryder 10/29/71
Akim Tamiroff........................ 10/29/01

October 30

John Adams 10/30/1735
Charles Atlas 10/30/1894
Herschel Bernardi 10/30/23
Dick Gautier 10/30/37
Ruth Gordon 10/30/1896
Harry Hamlin 10/30/51
Ruth Hussey 10/30/14
Louis Malle 10/30/32
Wallace Muhammad 10/30/33

Emily Post 10/30/1873
Ezar Pound 10/30/1885
Gus Savage 10/30/25
Grace Slick 10/30/39
Danny Tartabull 10/30/62
Henry Winkler 10/30/45
Michael Winner 10/30/35

October 31
Sara Allgood 10/31/1883
Barbara Bel-Geddes 10/31/22
John Candy 10/31/50
Blue Edwards 10/31/65
Dale Evans 10/31/12
Dick Francis 10/31/20
Lee Grant 10/31/30
Deidre Hall 10/31/49
Randy Jackson 10/31/61
Chiang Kai-Shek 10/31/1886
John Keats 10/31/1795
Michael Landon 10/31/36
Juliette Gorden Low 10/31/1860
Fred McGriff 10/31/63
Reza Pahlavi 10/31/60
Jane Pauley 10/31/50
Tom Paxton 10/31/37
Dan Rather 10/31/31
Roy Romer 10/31/28
Prince Norodom Sihanouk 10/31/22
David Ogden Stiers 10/31/42
Ether Waters 10/31/00

November 1
Max Adrian 11/1/03
Sholem Asch 11/1/1880
James Barton 11/1/1890
Barbara Bosson 11/1/39
Benvenuto Cellini 11/1/1500
Stephen Crane 11/1/1871
Victoria De Los Angeles 11/1/24
Larry Flynt 11/1/42
Robert Foxworth 11/1/41
A.R. Gurney, Jr. 11/1/30
James J. Kilpatrick 11/1/20

Lyle Lovett 11/1/57
Marcel Ophuls 11/1/27
Betsy Palmer 11/1/26
Gary Player 11/1/35
Henri Troyat 11/1/11
Fernando Valenzuela 11/1/60

November 2
Marie Antoinette 11/2/1755
Bernie Bickerstaff 11/2/43
Daniel Boone 11/2/1734
William Cullen Bryant 11/2/1794
Patrick Buchanan 11/2/38
Jean Baptise Chardin 11/2/1699
Paul Ford 11/2/01
Warren Harding 11/2/1865
Shere Hite 11/2/42
k.d. Lang 11/2/61
Burt Lancaster 11/2/13
Willie McGee 11/2/58
James Polk 11/2/1795
Stephanie Power 11/2/42
Ken Rosewall 11/2/34
Ann Rutherford 11/2/17
Warren Stevens 11/2/19
David Stockton 11/2/41
Luchino Visconti 11/2/06
Ray Walston 11/2/24
Dale Wasserman 11/2/17
Alfre Woodward 11/2/53

November 3
Adam Ant 11/3/54
Vincenzo Bellini 11/3/1801
Ken Berry 11/3/33
Jeremy Brett 11/3/35
Charles Bronson 11/3/22
Mike Dukakis 11/3/33
Mike Espy 11/3/53
Bob Feller 11/3/18
Bert Freed 11/3/19
Larry Gelman 11/3/30
Larry Holmes 11/3/49
Andre Malraux 11/3/01

Terrace McNally 11/3/39
Dennis Miller 11/3/54
James Reston 11/3/09
Roseanne 11/3/52
Yitzhak Shamir 11/3/14
Phil Simms 11/3/56
Lois Smith 11/3/30
Louis Sullivan 11/3/33
Bob Welch 11/3/56

November 4
Martin Balsam 11/4/19
Art Carney 11/4/18
Walter Cronkite 11/4/16
Paul Douglas 11/4/07
Will Hays 11/4/1885
Dixie Lee 11/4/11
Ralph Macchio 11/4/62
Isamu Noguchi 11/4/04
Doris Roberts 11/4/30
Auguste Rodin 11/4/1840
Will Rogers 11/4/1879
Loretta Swit 11/4/37
Pauline Trigere 11/4/12
Yanni 11/4/54
Gig Young 11/4/13

November 5
Eugene Debs 11/5/1855
Will Durant 11/5/1885
Art Garfunkel 11/5/41
Vivien Leigh 11/5/13
Arthur Liman 11/5/32
Jeb Stuart Magruder 11/5/34
Joel McCrea 11/5/06
John McGiver 11/5/13
Peter Noone 11/5/47
Tatum O'Neal 11/5/63
Roy Rogers 11/5/12
Sam Shepard 11/5/43
Ida Tarbell 11/5/1857
Ike Turner 11/5/31
Bill Walton 11/5/52
Mark West 11/5/60

November 6
Edward Debartolo, Jr. 11/6/46
Charles Henry Dow 11/6/1851
Pat Dye 11/6/39
John Falsey 11/6/51
Sally Field 11/6/46
Edsel Ford 11/6/1893
Glenn Frey 11/6/48
Juanita Hall 11/6/01
Walter Johnson 11/6/1887
James Jones 11/6/21
Lance Kerwin 11/6/60
Eric Krammer 11/6/64
James Naismith 11/6/1861
Mike Nichols 11/6/31
Ray Perkins 11/6/41
Jean Shrimpton 11/6/42
Maria Shriver 11/6/55
John Phillip Sousa 11/6/1854

November 7
Joey Bushin 11/7/16
Albert Camus 11/7/13
Madame Curie 11/7/1867
Billy Graham 11/7/18
Al Hirt 11/7/22
Dean Jagger 11/7/03
Al Martino 11/7/27
Joni Mitchell 11/7/43
Barry Newman 11/7/38
Joe Niekro 11/7/44
Tom Peters 11/7/42
Dana Plato 11/7/64
Johnny Rivers 11/7/42
Joan Sutherland 11/7/29
Mary Travers 11/7/37

November 8
Christiaan Barnard 11/8/22
Angel Cordero 11/8/42
Alain Delon 11/8/35
Leif Garrett 11/8/61
Edmund Halley 11/8/1656
Mary Hart 11/8/51

June Havoc 11/8/16
Christie Hefner 11/8/52
Katharine Hepburn 11/8/07
Rickie Lee Jones 11/8/54
Ira C. Magaziner 11/8/47
Walter Mirisch 11/8/21
Margaret Mitchell 11/8/00
Patti Page 11/8/27
Bonnie Raitt 11/8/49
Ester Rolle 11/8/33
Morley Safer 11/8/31
Robert Strauss 11/8/13
Leon Trotsky 11/8/1879

November 9

Spiro Agnew 11/9/18
Gail Borden 11/9/1801
Florence Chadwick 11/9/18
Marian Christy 11/9/32
Dorothy Dandridge 11/9/22
Marie Dressler 11/9/1869
Peter Drucker 11/9/09
Lou Ferrigno 11/9/52
Bob Gibson 11/9/35
Jerome Hines 11/9/21
Hedy Lamarr 11/9/14
Mae Marsh 11/9/1895
Claude Rains 11/9/1889
Carl Sagan 11/9/34
Sargent Shriver 11/9/15
Ivan Turgenev 11/9/1818
Tom Weiskopf 11/9/42
Ed Wynn 11/9/1886

November 10

Richard Burton 11/10/25
Donna Fargo 11/10/49
Martin Luther 11/10/1483
J.P. Marquand 11/10/1893
Mabel Normand 11/10/1897
MacKenzie Phillips 11/10/59
Alaina Reed 11/10/46
Ann Reinking 11/10/49
Jack Scalia 11/10/51

Roy Scheider 11/10/35

November 11

Maude Adams 11/11/1872
Bibi Anderson 11/11/35
Barbara Boxer 11/11/40
Rene Clair 11/11/1898
Fyodor Dostoevsky 11/11/1821
Howard Fast 11/11/14
Carlos Fuentes 11/11/28
Alger Hiss 11/11/04
Jack Jones 11/11/38
Charles Manson 11/11/34
Phillip McKeon 11/11/64
Demi Moore 11/11/62
Pat O'Brien 11/11/1899
George Patton 11/11/1885
William Proxmire 11/11/15
Robert Ryan 11/11/09
Sam Spiegel 11/11/01
Kurt Vonnegut, Jr. 11/11/22
Jonathan Winters 11/11/25
Fuzzy Zoeller 11/11/51

November 12

Ina Balin 11/12/37
Harry Blackmun 11/12/08
Alexander Borodin 11/12/1833
Nadia Comaneci 11/12/61
Joseph Coors 11/12/17
Kim Hunter 11/12/22
Princess Grace Kelly 11/12/29
Al Michaels 11/12/44
Jackie Oakie 11/12/03
Wallace Shawn 11/12/43
Jo Stafford 11/12/18
Dewitt Wallace 11/12/1889
Neil Young 11/12/45

November 13

Peter Arnett 11/13/34
Hermione Baddeley 11/13/06
Nathaniel Benchley 11/13/15
Louis Brandeis 11/13/1856

Linda Christian 11/13/23
John Drew 11/13/1853
Kevin Gamble 11/13/65
Whoopi Goldberg 11/13/55
Don Gordon 11/13/26
George V. Higgins 11/13/39
Joseph Hooker 11/13/1814
Joe Mantegna 11/13/47
Garry Marshall 11/13/34
Scott McNealy 11/13/54
Richard Mulligan 11/13/32
Alexander Scourby 11/13/13
Jean Seberg 11/13/38
Robert Louis Stevenson 11/13/1850
Vinny Testaverde 11/13/63
Oska Werner 11/13/22

November 14
Boutro Boutros-Ghali 11/14/22
Louise Brooks 11/14/06
Prince Charles 11/14/48
Aaron Copland 11/14/00
Rosemary Decamp 11/14/10
Johnny Desmond 11/14/21
Mamie Eisenhower 11/14/1896
Barbara Hutton 11/14/12
King Hussein of Jordan 11/14/35
Brian Keith 11/14/21
Veronica Lake 11/14/19
Claude Monet 11/14/1840
Leopold Mozart 11/14/1719
Jawaharlal Nehru 11/14/1889
Dick Powell 11/14/04
McLean Stevenson 11/14/29

November 15
Franklin P. Adams 11/15/1881
Greg Anthony 11/15/67
Ed Asner 11/15/29
Howard Baker 11/15/25
Daniel Barenboim 11/15/42
JoAnna Barnes 11/15/34
Carol Bruce 11/15/19
Petula Clark 11/15/32

Beverly D'Angelo 11/15/53
Felix Frankfurter 11/15/1882
John Kerr 11/15/31
Yaphet Kotto 11/15/44
Janet Lennon 11/15/46
Gen. Curtis LeMay 11/15/06
George O'Keeffee 11/15/1887
Erwin Rommel 11/15/1891
Joseph Wapner 11/15/19
Sam Waterston 11/15/40

November 16
Lisa Bonet 11/16/67
Elizabeth Drew 11/16/35
Zina Garrison 11/16/63
Dwight Gooden 11/16/64
W.C. Handy 11/16/1873
Paul Hindemith 11/16/1895
Joan Janis 11/16/26
George S. Kaufman 11/16/1889
Fibber McGee 11/16/1896
Burgess Meredith 11/16/08
Corey Pavin 11/16/59
Joanna Pettet 11/16/44
Martha Plimpton 11/16/70
Bebe Rebozo 11/16/12
Jo Jo White 11/16/46

November 17
Mischa Auer 11/17/05
Peter Cook 11/17/37
Danny Devito 11/17/44
Shelby Foote 11/17/16
Elvin Hayes 11/17/53
Rock Hudson 11/17/25
Lauren Hutton 11/17/44
Gordon Lightfoot 11/17/38
Mary Elizabeth Mastrantonio 11/17/58
Frank Maxwell 11/17/16
Cyril Ramaphosa 11/17/52
Martin Scorsese 11/17/42
Tom Seaver 11/17/44
Lee Strasberg 11/17/01

November 18

Imogene Coca	11/18/08
Dorothy Collins	11/18/26
Linda Evans	11/18/42
George Gallup	11/18/01
Raghib Ismail	11/18/69
Gene Mauch	11/18/25
Johnny Mercer	11/18/09
Cameron Mitchell	11/18/18
Warren Moon	11/18/56
Eugene Ormandy	11/18/1889
Ignace Paderewski	11/18/1860
Jameson Parker	11/18/48
Elizabeth Ann Perkins	11/18/60
Alan Shepard, Jr.	11/18/23
Susan Sullivan	11/18/45
Brenda Vaccaro	11/18/39

November 19

Alan Baxter	11/19/08
Roy Campanella	11/19/21
Dick Cavett	11/19/36
Tommy Dorsey	11/19/05
Jodie Foster	11/19/62
Indira Gandhi	11/19/17
James Garfield	11/19/1831
Dan Haggarty	11/19/41
Thomas Harkin	11/19/39
Larry King	11/19/33
Calvin Klein	11/19/42
Katy Moffatt	11/19/50
Ahmad Rashad	11/19/49
Meg Ryan	11/19/61
Ted Turner	11/19/38
Garrick Utley	11/19/39
Clifton Webb	11/19/1891
Alan Young	11/19/19

November 20

Duane Allman	11/20/46
Kaye Ballard	11/20/26
Joseph Biden	11/20/42
Robert Byrd	11/20/17
Judy Canova	11/20/16
Alistair Cooke	11/20/08
Franklin Cover	11/20/28
Richard Dawson	11/20/32
Bo Derek	11/20/56
Chester Gould	11/20/00
Veronica Hamel	11/20/45
Barbara Hendricks	11/20/48
Don January	11/20/29
Robert F. Kennedy	11/20/25
Evelyn Keys	11/20/19
Estelle Parsons	11/20/27
Maya Plisetskaya	11/20/25
Emilio Pucci	11/20/14
Dick Smothers	11/20/38
Phyllis Thaxter	11/20/21
Gene Tierney	11/20/20
Judy Woodruff	11/20/46
Sean Young	11/20/59

November 21

Troy Aikman	11/21/66
Vivian Blaine	11/21/24
Paul Bogart	11/21/19
Joseph Campanella	11/21/27
Marcia Carsey	11/21/44
Marilyn French	11/21/29
Ken Griffey, Jr.	11/21/69
Goldie Hawn	11/21/45
David Hemmings	11/21/41
Dr. John	11/21/40
Reggie Lewis	11/21/65
Laurence Luckingbill	11/21/34
Rene Magritte	11/21/1898
Natalia Makarova	11/21/40
Ralph Meeker	11/21/20
Earl Monroe	11/21/44
Stan Musial	11/21/20
Eleanor Powell	11/21/11
Harold Ramis	11/21/44
Sal Salvador	11/21/25
Nicollette Sheridan	11/21/61
Marlo Thomas	11/21/43
Majorie Vincent	11/21/64

Voltaire 11/21/1694

November 22
Eric Allen.................................. 11/22/65
Boris Becker 11/22/67
Guion Bluford 11/22/42
Michael Callan........................ 11/22/35
Hoagy Carmichael 11/22/1899
Tom Conti 11/22/41
Jamie Lee Curtis 11/22/58
Rodney Dangerfield 11/22/21
Charles DeGaulle 11/22/1890
Doris Duke 11/22/12
James Edwards 11/22/55
Allen Garfield 11/22/39
Andre Gide 11/22/1869
Terry Gilliam 11/22/40
Mariel Hemingway 11/22/61
Arthur Hiller........................... 11/22/23
Mary Jackson 11/22/10
Billy Jean King 11/22/43
Geraldine Page 11/22/24
Clairborne Pell........................ 11/22/18
Wiley Post 11/22/00
Dick Stockton 11/22/42
Robert Vaughn 11/22/32

November 23
Billy the Kid 11/23/1859
Maxwell Caufield 11/23/59
Ellen Drew 11/23/15
Jose Duarte 11/23/26
Bruce Hornsby 11/23/54
Victor Jory 11/23/03
Boris Karloff........................... 11/23/1887
Sam Keen 11/23/31
"Harpo" Marx 11/23/1893

November 24
Dave Bing................................ 11/24/43
William F. Buckley, Jr. 11/24/25
Dale Carnegie 11/24/1888
Ron Dellums 11/24/35
Henri de Toulouse-Lautrec 11/24/1864

Howard Duff 11/24/17
Geraldine Fitzgerald............... 11/24/14
Marlin Fitzwater 11/24/42
Corinne Griffith................... 11/24/1896
Scott Joplin 11/24/1868
Garson Kanin........................... 11/24/12
John V. Lindsay 11/24/21
"Lucky" Luciano 11/24/1897
Bat Masterson 11/24/1853
Carry Nation........................ 11/24/1846
Cathleen Nesbitt 11/24/1889
Oscar Robertson 11/24/38
Alfred Schnittke 11/24/34
Paul Tagliabue......................... 11/24/40
Zachary Taylor 11/24/1784

November 25
Steve Brodie 11/25/19
Cris Carter............................... 11/25/65
Kathryn Crosby 11/25/33
Bucky Dent 11/25/51
Joe Dimaggio 11/25/14
Helen Gahagan Douglas 11/25/00
Martin Feldstein 11/25/39
Joe Gibbs 11/25/40
Amy Grant 11/25/60
Kathryn Grant 11/25/33
Jeffery Hunter.......................... 11/25/27
John Kennedy, Jr. 11/25/60
Bernie Kosar 11/25/63
John Larroquette 11/25/47
John McVie 11/25/45
Ricardo Montalban 11/25/20
Virgil Thomson 11/25/1896

November 26
Charles Brackett 11/26/1892
Robert Goulet 11/26/33
John Harvard 11/26/1607
Eugene Ionesco 11/26/12
Eugene Istomin 11/26/25
Shawn Kemp 11/26/69
Rich Little 11/26/38
Marian Mercer......................... 11/26/35

Daniel Mannix Petrie 11/26/20
Samuel Reshevsky 11/26/11
Charles Schulz 11/26/22
Eric Sevareid 11/26/12
Art Shell 11/26/46
Tina Turner 11/26/39
Emlyn Williams 11/26/05

November 27

James Agee 11/27/09
Hall Bartlett 11/27/29
Robin Givens 11/27/64
Jimi Hendrix 11/27/42
Caroline Kennedy 11/27/57
Bruce Lee 11/27/40
David Merrick 11/27/12
Eddie Rabbitt 11/27/41
William Simon 11/27/27
Marshall Thompson 11/27/25
Jaleel White 11/27/76

November 28

Brooks Atkinson 11/28/1894
William Blake 11/28/1757
James O. Eastland 11/28/04
Friedrich Engels 11/28/1820
Alexander Godunov 11/28/49
Berry Gordy, Jr. 11/28/29
Gloria Grahame 11/28/25
Ed Harris 11/28/50
Gary Hart 11/28/36
Jose Iturbi 11/28/1895
Hope Lange 11/28/38
Alberto Moravia 11/28/07
Judd Nelson 11/28/59
Randy Newman 11/28/43
Michael Ritchie 11/28/38
Anton Rubenstein 11/28/1829
Paul Shaffer 11/28/49
Roy Tarpley 11/28/64
Paul Warfield 11/28/42
Matt Williams 11/28/65

November 29

Busby Berkeley 11/29/1895
Dee Brown 11/29/68
Suzy Chaffee 11/29/46
John Gary 11/29/32
Petra Kelly 11/29/47
Diane Ladd 11/29/32
Howie Mandell 11/29/55
Chuck Mangione 11/29/40
Jamal Mashburn 11/29/72
Willie Morris 11/29/34
Adam Clayton Powell, Jr. 11/29/08
David Reuben 11/29/33
Vin Scully 11/29/27
Garry Shandling 11/29/49
Paul Simon (Senator) 11/29/28
Merle Travis 11/29/17

November 30

Shirley Chisholm 11/30/24
Winston Churchill 11/30/1874
Dick Clark 11/30/29
Joan Ganz Cooney 11/30/29
Richard Crenna 11/30/27
Angier Biddle Duke 11/30/15
Roger Glover 11/30/45
Robert Guillaume 11/30/37
Abbie Hoffman 11/30/36
Billy Idol 11/30/55
Bo Jackson 11/30/62
G. Gordon Liddy 11/30/30
David Mamet 11/30/45
Virginia Mayo 11/30/20
Gordon Parks 11/30/12
Mandy Patinkin 11/30/52
Allan Sherman 11/30/24
Jonathan Swift 11/30/1667
Mark Twain 11/30/1835
Bill Walsh 11/30/31
Paul Westphal 11/30/50
Efrem Zimbalist, Jr. 11/30/23

December 1

Woody Allen	12/1/35
Carol Alt	12/1/60
John Densmore	12/1/44
David Doyle	12/1/25
George Foster	12/1/48
Dianne Lennon	12/1/39
Mary Martin	12/1/14
Bette Midler	12/1/45
Gilbert O'Sullivan	12/1/46
Richard Pryor	12/1/40
Lou Rawls	12/1/36
Cyril Ritchard	12/1/1897
Kurt Schmoke	12/1/49
Dick Shaw	12/1/23
Charlene Tilton	12/1/58
Lee Trevino	12/1/39
Treat Williams	12/1/51
Dennis Wilson	12/1/41

December 2

Merrill Ashley	12/2/50
Maria Callas	12/2/23
Hy Gardner	12/2/04
Adolph Green	12/2/15
Alexander Haig	12/2/24
Julie Harris	12/2/25
Charles Ringling	12/2/1863
Monica Seles	12/2/73
George Seurat	12/2/1859
Ezra Stone	12/2/17
Gianni Versace	12/2/46

December 3

Mary Alice	12/3/41
Bobby Allison	12/3/37
Jim Backus	12/3/24
Joseph Conrad	12/3/1857
Hendrik Conscience	12/3/1812
Phyllis Curtin	12/3/27
Anna Freud	12/3/1895
Jean-Luc Godard	12/3/30
Daryl Hannah	12/3/61
George B. McClellan	12/3/1826

Rick Mears	12/3/51
Ozzy Osbourne	12/3/48
Larry Parks	12/3/14
Jim Plunkett	12/3/47
Gilbert Stuart	12/3/1755
Andy Williams	12/3/30
Katarina Witt	12/3/66

December 4

Jeff Blake	12/4/70
Horst Buchholz	12/4/33
"Pappy" Boyington	12/4/06
Jeff Bridges	12/4/49
Lee Dorsey	12/4/26
Deanna Durbin	12/4/21
Francisco Franco	12/4/1866
Buck Jones	12/4/1889
Wassily Kandinsky	12/4/1866
Bernard King	12/4/56
Chelsea Noble	12/4/64
Alex North	12/4/10
Lillian Russell	12/4/1861
Lee Smith	12/4/57
Marisa Tomei	12/4/64
Patricia Wettig	12/4/51
Dennis Wilson	12/4/44

December 5

Morgan Brittany	12/5/51
Jose Carreras	12/5/46
George Armstrong Custer	12/5/1839
Joan Didion	12/5/35
Walt Disney	12/5/01
Arnold Gingrich	12/5/03
Carrie Hamilton	12/5/63
Nunnally Johnson	12/5/1897
Larry Kert	12/5/30
Fritz Lang	12/5/1890
Chad Mitchell	12/5/36
Art Monk	12/5/57
Otto Preminger	12/5/06
Strom Thurmond	12/5/02
Calvin Trillin	12/5/35
Martin Van Buren	12/5/1782

Lanny Wadkins 12/5/49
John Williams 12/5/25

December 6

Hardie Albright 12/6/03
Steve Bedrosian 12/6/57
Larry Bowa 12/6/45
David Brubeck 12/6/20
Wally Cox 12/6/24
Eve Curie 12/6/04
Frederick Duesenbery 12/6/1876
Lynn Fontanne 12/6/1887
Ira Gershwin 12/6/1896
Otto Graham 12/6/21
William S. Hart 12/6/1872
Tom Hulce 12/6/53
Don King 12/6/32
Agnes Moorehead 12/6/06
James Naughton 12/6/45
Dwight Stone 12/6/53
Janine Turner 12/6/62
Bobby Van 12/6/32
Steven Wright 12/6/55

December 7

Fay Bainter 12/7/1892
Johnny Bench 12/7/47
Gian Lorenzo Bernini 12/7/1598
Larry Bird 12/7/56
Ellen Burstyn 12/7/32
Roy Cameron 12/7/12
Willa Cather 12/7/1873
Harry Chapin 12/7/42
Thad Cochran 12/7/37
Rudolf Frimi 12/7/1879
Ted Knight 12/7/23
Reginald Lewis 12/7/42
Louis Prima 12/7/12
Mary, Queen of Scots 12/7/1542
Richard Warren Sears 12/7/1863
Carole Simpson 12/7/40
Tom Waits 12/7/49
Eli Wallach 12/7/15
Bob Weiss 12/7/18

December 8

Greg Allman 12/8/47
Kim Basinger 12/8/53
Jerry Butler 12/8/39
David Carradine 12/8/36
Lee J. Cobb 12/8/11
Sammy Davis, Jr. 12/8/25
Richard Fleischer 12/8/16
James Galway 12/8/39
Jane Garrison 12/8/51
Oswald Jacoby 12/8/02
James MacArthur 12/8/37
Jim Morrison 12/8/43
Sinead O'Connor 12/8/66
Diego Rivera 12/8/1886
John Rubinstein 12/8/46
Maximilian Schell 12/8/30
Lawrence Schiller 12/8/36
E.C. Segar 12/8/1894
Marc Siegel 12/8/16
James Thurber 12/8/1894
Eli Whitney 12/8/1765
Flip Wilson 12/8/33

December 9

Joan Armatrading 12/9/50
Al "Bubba" Baker 12/9/56
Beau Bridges 12/9/41
Dick Butkus 12/9/42
John Cassavetes 12/9/29
Broderick Crawford 12/9/11
Kirk Douglas 12/9/16
Morton Downey, Jr. 12/9/33
Douglas Fairbanks, Jr 12/9/09
Redd Foxx 12/9/22
World B Free 12/9/53
Hermione Gingold 12/9/1897
Margaret Hamilton 12/9/02
Bill Hartack 12/9/32
Buck Henry 12/9/30
C. Thomas Howell 12/9/66
Emmett Kelly 12/9/1898
Tom Kite 12/9/49
John Malkovich 12/9/53

Dina Merrill 12/9/25
John Milton 12/9/1608
Michael Nouri 12/9/46
Tip O'Neill 12/9/12
Donny Osmond 12/9/57
Dalton Trumbo 12/9/05
Dick Van Patten 12/9/28

December 10

Mark Aguirre........................... 12/10/59
Kenneth Branagh 12/10/60
Susan Dey 12/10/52
Emily Dickinson 12/10/1830
Fionnula Flanagan 12/10/41
William Lloyd Garrison 12/10/1805
Harold Gould 12/10/23
Morton Gould 12/10/13
Chet Huntley 12/10/11
Dorothy Lamour 12/10/14
Gloria Loring 12/10/46
Una Merkel 12/10/03
Clayton Yeutter 12/10/30

December 11

Bess Armstrong 12/11/53
Hector Berlioz...................... 12/11/1803
Betsy Blair 12/11/23
Doc Blanchard 12/11/24
Elliot Carter............................ 12/11/08
Ron Carey 12/11/35
Terri Garr 12/11/49
Linda Day George.................. 12/11/46
Tom Hayden............................ 12/11/39
Mike Henneman 12/11/61
Jermaine Jackson 12/11/54
Stu Jackson 12/11/55
John Kerry............................... 12/11/43
Fiorello La Guadia 12/11/1882
Brenda Lee 12/11/44
Michael McCaskey.................. 12/11/43
Victor McLaglen.................. 12/11/1886
Donna Mills 12/11/43
Rita Moreno 12/11/31
Christina Onassis 12/11/50

Carlo Ponti 12/11/13
Gilbert Roland 12/11/05
Susan Seidelman 12/11/52
Alexander Solzhenitsyn 12/11/18
Jean-Louis Trintingnant 12/11/30

December 12

Tracy Austin 12/12/62
Bob Barker............................... 12/12/23
Dicky Betts 12/12/43
Mayim Bialik 12/12/75
Laura Hope Crews.............. 12/12/1879
Sheila E. 12/12/58
Emerson Fittipaldi 12/12/46
Gustave Flaubert................. 12/12/1821
Connie Francis........................ 12/12/38
Arthur Garfield Hayes 12/12/1881
Curt Jurgens............................ 12/12/15
Ed Koch 12/12/24
Marie Louise 12/12/1791
Og Mandino............................ 12/12/23
Pete O'Malley 12/12/37
Cathy Rigby 12/12/52
Edward G. Robinson 12/12/1893
Frank Sinatra 12/12/15
Dionne Warwick 12/12/41
Grover Washington, Jr. 12/12/43
Joe Williams 12/12/18

December 13

Marc Connelly 12/13/1890
John Davidson......................... 12/13/41
Richard Dent........................... 12/13/60
Larry Doby............................... 12/13/24
Sergei Fedorov 12/13/69
Van Heflin................................ 12/13/10
Ferguson Jenkins..................... 12/13/43
Mary Todd Lincoln............. 12/13/1818
Carlos Montgomery 12/13/03
Carlos Montoya...................... 12/13/03
Archie Moore........................... 12/13/13
Ted Nugent.............................. 12/13/49
Randy Owen 12/13/49
Larry Parks 12/13/14

Drew Pearson 12/13/1897
Christopher Plummer 12/13/29
Robert Joseph Prosky 12/13/30
Lillian Roth 12/13/10
George Shultz 12/13/20
Don Taylor 12/13/20
Dick Van Dyke 12/13/25
Johnny Whitaker 12/13/59
Richard Zanuck 12/13/34

December 14
Morey Amsterdam 12/14/14
Ib Andersen 12/14/54
Bill Buckner............................ 12/14/49
Dan Dailey 12/14/15
Gen. James Doolittle 12/14/1896
Patty Duke 12/14/46
George Furth 12/14/32
Don Hewitt 12/14/22
Spike Jones 12/14/11
Abbe Lane 12/14/32
Anthony Mason 12/14/66
Michael Ovitz 12/14/46
Lee Remick.............................. 12/14/35
Charlie Rich 12/14/32
Margaret Chase Smith 12/14/1897
Stan Smith 12/14/46
Clark Terry............................. 12/14/20
Hal Williams 12/14/38

December 15
Maxwell Anderson 12/15/1888
Jerry Ball................................ 12/15/64
Nick Buoniconti 12/15/40
James E. Carter 12/15/24
Jeff Chandler.......................... 12/15/18
Dave Clark 12/15/42
Tim Conway 12/15/33
Alexandre Eiffel 12/15/1832
J. Paul Getty 12/15/1892
Don Johnson 12/15/49
Karen Morrow 12/15/36
Nero 12/15/37AD
Eddie Palmieri 12/15/36

Helen Slater 12/15/63

December 16
Jane Austin........................... 12/16/1775
Ludwig van Beethoven 12/16/1770
Steve Bochco 12/16/43
Arthur Clarke 12/16/17
Noel Coward 12/16/1899
Ben Cross 12/16/47
Morris S. Dees, Jr.................... 12/16/36
Frank Deford 12/16/38
John Jacob 12/16/34
Margaret Mead...................... 12/16/01
William Perry 12/16/62
George Santayana 12/16/1863
George Schaefer 12/16/20
Lesley Stahl 12/16/41
Liv Ullman 12/16/39

December 17
Erskine Caldwell.................... 12/17/03
Arthur Fiedler 12/17/1894
Mike Gottfried 12/17/44
Bob Guccione.......................... 12/17/30
Eugene Levy 12/17/46
Cal Ripken, Sr. 12/17/35
William Roerick 12/17/12
William Safire 12/17/29
Tommy Steele 12/17/36
Patrice Wymore...................... 12/17/26

December 18
Willy Brandt 12/18/13
Abe Burrows 12/18/10
Ramsey Clark 12/18/27
Ty Cobb 12/18/1893
Jules Dassin............................ 12/18/11
Ozzie Davis 12/18/17
Francis Ferdinand 12/18/1863
Betty Grable 12/18/16
Fletch Henderson................ 12/18/1897
Hal Kanter.............................. 12/18/18
Paul Klee 12/18/1879
Greg Landry 12/18/46

Ray Liotta 12/18/55
Leonard Maltin........................ 12/18/50
Ray Meyer 12/18/13
Charles Oakley 12/18/63
Brain Orser.............................. 12/18/61
Brad Pitt.................................. 12/18/64
Keith Richards 12/18/43
Gene Shue 12/18/31
Roger Smith 12/18/32
Steven Spielberg...................... 12/18/47
George Stevens........................ 12/18/04

December 19
Jennifer Beals 12/19/63
Leonid Brezhnev 12/19/06
Dr. William DeVries 12/19/43
Janie Fricke............................. 12/19/47
Jean Genet 12/19/10
Gordon Jackson 12/19/23
Al Kaline 12/19/34
Jeanne Kirkpatrick 12/19/26
Oliver La Farge....................... 12/19/01
Bobby Layne............................ 12/19/26
Richard Leakey 12/19/44
Limmahl 12/19/58
Kevin McHale.......................... 12/19/57
Alyssa Milano.......................... 12/19/73
Miguel Pinero 12/19/46
Edmond Purdom 12/19/24
Tim Reid.................................. 12/19/44
Fritz Reiner 12/19/1888
Ralph Richardson 12/19/02
Robert Sherman....................... 12/19/25
David Susskind 12/19/20
Alberto Tamba 12/19/66
Cicely Tyson 12/19/33
Robert Urich 12/19/47
Maurice White......................... 12/19/41
Reggie White 12/19/61

December 20
Jenny Agutter 12/20/52
Pamela Austin 12/20/41
Albert Dekker.......................... 12/20/05

Irene Dunne 12/20/04
Uri Geller................................ 12/20/46
Gordon Getty........................... 12/20/33
George Roy Hill 12/20/22
John Hillerman........................ 12/20/32
Sidney Hook 12/20/02
Max Lerner.............................. 12/20/02
Nate Newton 12/20/61
Mala Powers 12/20/31
Ann Richards (Actress) 12/20/18
Branch Rickey 12/20/1881
Audrey Totter.......................... 12/20/18

December 21
Joaquin Andujar...................... 12/21/52
Phil Donahue........................... 12/21/35
Benjamin Disraeli 12/21/1804
Chris Evert 12/21/54
Jane Fonda 12/21/37
Josh Gibson 12/21/11
Florence Griffith-Joyner 12/21/59
Masaccio 12/21/1401
Terry Mills 12/21/67
Ed Nelson................................ 12/21/28
Jean Racine 12/21/1639
Joe Paterno 12/21/26
Kiefer Sutherland.................... 12/21/67
Michael Tilson Thomas 12/21/44
Andy Van Slyke 12/21/60
Kurt Waldheim 12/21/18
Carl Wilson 12/21/46
Paul Winchell 12/21/23
Frank Zappa 12/21/40

December 22
Peggy Ashcroft 12/22/07
Barbara Billingsley................. 12/22/22
Steve Carlton 12/22/44
Hector Elizondo 12/22/36
Ralph Fiennes 12/22/62
Steve Garvey............................ 12/22/48
Maurice Gibb 12/22/49
Robin Gibb 12/22/49
Lady Bird Johnson 12/22/12

Andre Kostelanetz 12/22/01
Connie Mack (Baseball) 12/22/1862
Giacomo Puccini 12/22/1858
Gene Rayburn 12/22/17
Ruth Roman 12/22/24
Diane Sawyer 12/22/45
Jan Stephenson 12/22/51
Edgar Varese 12/22/1885
Jim Wright 12/22/22

December 23

Emperor Akihito 12/23/33
Alexander I 12/23/1777
Jose Greco 12/23/18
James Gregory 12/23/11
Harry Guardino 12/23/25
Corey Haim 12/23/71
Elizabeth Hartman 12/23/41
Paul Hornung 12/23/35
Yousef Karsh 12/23/08
Susan Lucci 12/23/46
Bill Rodgers 12/23/47
Vincent Sardi 12/23/1885
Helmut Schmidt 12/23/18
Madam C.J. Walker 12/23/1867
Dick Weber 12/23/29

December 24

Jill Bennett 12/24/31
Kit Carson 12/24/1809
Mary Higgins Clark 12/24/31
Michael Curtiz 12/24/1898
Sharon Farrell 12/24/49
Ava Gardner 12/24/22
Howard Hughes 12/24/05
Robert Joffrey 12/24/30
Mike Mazurki 12/24/09
Woody Shaw 12/24/44

December 25

Clara Barton 12/25/1821
Humphrey Bogart 12/25/1899
Jimmy Buffett 12/25/46
Cab Calloway 12/25/07

Jesus Christ .... 12/25/4 BC
Clark Clifford 12/25/06
Quentin Crisp 12/25/08
Larry Csonka 12/25/46
Nellie Fox 12/25/27
Rickey Henderson 12/25/58
Conrad Hilton 12/25/1887
Kelly Isley 12/25/37
Gene Lemont 12/25/46
Annie Lennox 12/25/54
Little Richard 12/25/35
Barton MacLane 12/25/02
Barbara Mandrell 12/25/48
Tony Martin 12/25/13
Ismail Merchant 12/25/36
C.C.H. Pounder 12/25/52
Robert Ripley 12/25/1893
Anwar el Sadat 12/25/18
Gary Sandy 12/25/45
Rod Serling 12/25/24
Moses Soyer 12/25/1899
Ralph Soyer 12/25/1899
Sissy Spacek 12/25/49
Ken Stabler 12/25/45
Maurice Utrillo 12/25/1883
Rebecca West 12/25/1892

December 26

Steve Allen 12/26/21
Elisha Cook, Jr. 12/26/06
Carlton Fisk 12/26/47
Alan King 12/26/27
Doris Lilly 12/26/26
Henry Miller 12/26/1891
Donald Moffat 12/26/30
Regine 12/26/29
Ozzie Smith 12/26/54
Phil Spector 12/26/36
Mao Tse-Tung 12/26/1893
Richard Widmark 12/26/14

December 27

John Amos 12/27/41
Moshe Arens 12/27/25

Anne Armstrong 12/27/27
Karla Bonoff 12/27/52
Gerard Depardieu 12/27/48
Marlene Dietrich 12/27/01
Tovah Feldshuh 12/27/52
Sydney Greenstreet 12/27/1879
Barnard Lanvin 12/27/35
Oscar LeVant 12/27/06
David Marr 12/27/33
Dr. William Masters 12/27/15
Tracy Nelson 12/27/44
Louis Pasteur 12/27/1822
Arthur Penhallon 12/27/52
Cokie Roberts 12/27/43

December 28

Cliff Arquette 12/28/05
Lew Ayres 12/28/08
Owen Bieber 12/28/29
Lee Bowman 12/28/14
Joe Diffie 12/28/58
Hubert Green 12/28/46
Earl Fatha Hines 12/28/05
Lou Jacobi 12/28/13
Nigel Kennedy 12/28/56
Ray Knight 12/28/52
Sam Levenson 12/28/11
Martin Milner 12/28/27
Hildegarde Neff 12/28/25
Simon Raven 12/28/27
Maggie Smith 12/28/34
Everson Walls 12/28/59
Denzel Washington 12/28/54
Woodrow Wilson 12/28/1856
Edgar Winter 12/28/46
Mao Zedong 12/28/1893

December 29

Jules Bledsoe 12/29/1898
Tom Bradley 12/29/17
Pablo Casals 12/29/1876
Ted Danson 12/29/47
Marianne Faithfull 12/29/46
Joe Gilliam 12/29/50

Charles Goodyear 12/29/1800
Wayne H. Huizenga 12/29/39
Tom Jarriel 12/29/44
Andrew Johnson 12/29/1808
Gelsey Kirkland 12/29/52
Bert Leighton 12/29/1877
Viveca Lindfors 12/29/20
Ray Nitschke 12/29/36
Robert Ruark 12/29/15
Mary Tyler Moore 12/29/37
Jon Voight 12/29/38
Jess Willard 12/29/1881

December 30

June Anderson 12/30/52
Suzy Bogguss 12/30/56
James Burrows 12/30/40
Bo Diddley 12/30/28
Ben Johnson (Athlete) 12/30/61
Davey Jones 12/30/46
Dmitri Kabalevsky 12/30/04
Rudyard Kipling 12/30/1865
Sandy Koufax 12/30/35
Jack Lord 12/30/30
Jeff Lynne 12/30/42
Dennis Morgan 12/30/10
Michael Nesmith 12/30/42
Jeannette Nolan 12/30/11
Bert Parks 12/30/14
Carol Reed 12/30/06
Paul Stookey 12/30/37
Russ Tamblyn 12/30/35
Hideki Tojo 12/30/1884
Tracey Ullman 12/30/59
Jo Van Fleet 12/30/19
Marie Wilson 12/30/16

December 31

Elizabeth Arden 12/31/1884
Giovanni Boldini 12/31/1842
Joe Dallesando 12/31/48
John Denver 12/31/43
Anthony Hopkins 12/31/37
Val Kilmer 12/31/59

Ben Kingsley 12/31/43
George C. Marshall 12/31/1880
Tim Matheson 12/31/48
Henri Matisse 12/31/1869
Sarah Miles 12/31/43
Nathan Milstein 12/31/04
Pola Negri 12/31/1894
Odetta 12/31/30
Patti Smith.............................. 12/31/46
Jule Styne 12/31/05
Donna Summer 12/31/48
Andy Summers 12/31/42
Diane Von Furstenberg 12/31/46

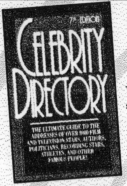